'ORRIBLE BRITISH TRUE CRIME

VOLUME FOUR

Ben Oakley

TITLES BY BEN OAKLEY

FICTION

HARRISON LAKE INVESTIGATIONS
The Camden Killer
The Limehouse Hotel
Monster of the Algarve

HONEYSUCKLE GOODWILLIES
The Mystery of Grimlow Forest
The Mystery of Crowstones Island

SUBNET SF TRILOGY
Unknown Origin
Alien Network
Final Contact

NONFICTION

TRUE CRIME
Bizarre True Crime Series
Orrible British True Crime Series
The Monstrous Book of Serial Killers
True Crime 365 series
Year of the Serial Killer

OTHER NONFICTION
The Immortal Hour: The True Story of Netta Fornario
Suicide Prevention Handbook

Look for more in the Orrible British True Crime Series!

OUT NOW!

Copyright © 2022 Ben Oakley.

First published in 2022 by Twelvetrees Camden.

This edition 2022.

The right of Ben Oakley to be identified as the
Author of the Work has been asserted by him in accordance
with the Copyright, Designs and Patents Act 1988.

Visit the author's website at www.benoakley.co.uk

All rights reserved. No part of this book may be reproduced, or stored in a retrieval system, or transmitted in any form or by any means, electronic, mechanical, photocopying, recording, or otherwise, without express written permission of the publisher.

Each case has been fully researched and fact-checked to bring you the best stories possible and all information is correct at the time of publication. This book is meant for entertainment and informational purposes only.

While the publisher and author have used their best efforts in preparing this book, they make no representations or warranties with respect to the accuracy or completeness of the contents of this book. Neither the publisher nor the author shall be liable for any loss of profit or any other commercial damages, including but not limited to special, incidental, consequential, personal, or other damages.

The author or publisher cannot be held responsible for any errors or misinterpretation of the facts detailed within. The book is not intended to hurt or defame individuals or companies involved.

ISBN: 978-1-7397149-7-0

Cover design by Ben Oakley.

For information about special discounts available
for bulk purchases, sales promotions, book signings,
trade shows, and distribution, contact
sales@twelvetreescamden.com

Twelvetrees Camden Ltd
71-75 Shelton Street, Covent Garden
London, WC2H 9JQ

www.twelvetreescamden.com

Orrible British True Crime Volume 4

The London Nail Bombings 11

The Ice Cream Wars 23

The Pendle Witches 31

The Playboy Bunny and the Schoolgirl Murders ... 41

The Wardell Murder 51

Britain's Youngest Serial Killer 61

The Camden Ripper 69

Umbrella Murder 79

Brighton Babes in the Wood 87

The Brink's-Mat Robbery 97

The Hungerford Massacre 111

Saturday Night Strangler 123

The Monster Butler & The Sidekick 133

The West's 141

Exorcism Turned Loving Husband into Killer 153

From the 17th Century to the 21st, a bonanza collection of British true crime stories covering murder, serial killers, robbery, gangs, and witchcraft!

1. London Nail Bombings

Across a two-week period in the Spring of 1999, three nail bombs exploded across London, leaving three dead and 140 injured, and a suspect who wanted to set fire to the country and start a race war.

2. The Ice Cream Wars

In 1980s Glasgow, rival criminal gangs were using ice cream vans to sell drugs and stolen goods, leading to the mass murder of six people and a man gluing himself to the railings of Buckingham Palace.

3. The Pendle Witches

In the summer of 1612, ten witches, six from two rival families, were found guilty of murder and witchcraft and executed at Gallows Hill, in one of the best-recorded witch trials in history.

4. The Playboy Bunny and the Schoolgirl Murders

A Playboy Bunny and a schoolgirl were attacked and killed in two separate incidents in London six months apart, by the same killer who has never been identified.

5. The Wardell Murder

After a body of a woman was found near a motorway, police rushed to her home to find her husband bound and gagged, claiming they were attacked by a man in a clown mask – but a twist this way comes.

6. Britain's Youngest Serial Killer

A 15-year-old boy claiming he was possessed by the Devil and heard voices telling him to kill, stabbed to death two people and was caught while planning a third.

7. The Camden Ripper

A devil-worshipping serial killer brutally murdered and dismembered at least three sex workers before dumping their body parts in canals and bins around Camden.

8. Umbrella Murder

While walking across Waterloo Bridge, a Bulgarian writer and journalist was assassinated after being stabbed in the thigh with the poisonous tip of an umbrella, by an assassin codenamed Piccadilly.

9. Brighton Babes in the Wood

Two nine-year-old girls were lured to their deaths by a monster who escaped justice for 32 years due to errors in the way forensics handled the original evidence.

10. The Brink's-Mat Robbery

A gang of armed robbers stole £26milllion of gold bullion, causing a trail of bloodshed and stupidity, in which only two men were convicted of direct involvement, with much of the gold still missing.

11. The Hungerford Massacre

In one of the deadliest mass shootings in Britain, a lone wolf went on a day-long spree, killing 16 people and leaving a quaint English market town looking like a war zone, in a case that changed gun laws.

12. Saturday Night Strangler

A Welsh serial killer who raped and killed three girls in Port Talbot in 1973 on Saturday nights, was caught 30 years later – after his death – in the first case in history solved using familial DNA testing.

13. The Monster Butler & The Sidekick

Scottish serial killer Archibald Hall, known as The Monster Butler, killed five people in the late 1970s while working for the British upper class, with help from his sidekick, Kitto.

14. The West's

A cruel tale of serial killing, abuse, and Britain's most evil couple, Fred and Rose West, who buried the bodies of their victims under the patio in their garden.

15. Exorcism Turned Loving Husband into Killer

A loving husband, thought to be possessed by 40 demons, became the subject of an all-night exorcism, and less than two hours later; ripped his wife and dog to pieces with his bare hands.

The London Nail Bombings

Across a two-week period in the Spring of 1999, three nail bombs exploded across London, leaving three dead and 140 injured, and a suspect who wanted to set fire to the country and start a race war.

In the late afternoon of Saturday 17th April 1999, as many people were walking through Brixton Market in Electric Avenue, London, a loud, deafening blast, like a huge gust of wind blew out the windows from surrounding buildings. A bomb, containing thousands of four-inch nails had exploded, injuring 48 people.

It was the start of a bombing campaign that left three people dead and 140 people physically injured with four people losing limbs. In the aftermath of the Brixton bombing, people were found lying on the ground screaming for help, with one man having suffered glass wounds and over 30 nails embedded in his legs.

A two-year-old boy was left with a nail lodged in his brain, as the force of the explosion had sent the nail flying towards his head. X-rays showed the nail was completely embedded in his head but fortunately the boy survived after an operation was successful in removing it.

In a bizarre twist of fate, the bomb could have been prevented from going off. The bomb was made by using explosives from fireworks which were taped inside a sports bag. Traders at the market, noticed a man acting suspiciously when he dropped the bag at the back of one of the market stalls in the busiest section of the street.

One of the traders moved the bag to a less-crowded area and called police but two other traders moved it again, worried about what was inside. A 5.25pm, as police were closing in on the markets, one of the traders opened the bag, and the bomb went off. The explosion was so powerful, it destroyed a car on the other side of the street.

Brick Lane

1999 Britain was a little different than it is today, and at the time, immediate suspicion fell on the IRA (Provisional Irish Republican Army), who had been responsible for various bombings throughout the country over the years. Yet, the style of bomb and location it had gone off, discounted the IRA from the attack. Suspicion then fell on right-wing terrorists but none could be found.

Two days later, the neo-Nazi terrorist group, Combat 18, claimed responsibility in a phone call to police and the press. Combat 18 was founded in 1992 by the British National Party (BNP) to protect its events from anti-fascists. The group were later linked to various deaths of immigrants and non-whites and are said to still have links to similar groups in Canada.

The claim of Combat 18 was discounted by police almost immediately as a false one – which it was. The police ploughed through miles of CCTV footage on videotape attempting to track the bomber. Investigators then suspected the motive of the attack was racism, due to Brixton's importance for the African-Caribbean community.

A week later, on Saturday 24th April, the bomber struck again in Brick Lane, in the East End of London. The main market in Brick Lane, an area known as the capital of the Bangladeshi community, is on a Sunday but the bomber mistakenly thought it was on a Saturday. The similarly created bomb was placed in a Reebok sports bag and placed near a wall close to the markets on Hanbury Street.

A local man spotted the bag and assumed it was lost property, so he placed it in the boot of his car and went to the local police station which was shut. The man then parked his car outside number 42 Brick Lane. While he was on the phone to police, the bomb exploded and injured 13 people, severely damaged several vehicles, and blew out the windows of many buildings along the street.

London was on edge

Had the bomb been left at its location on the Sunday, and not been spotted, then it may have resulted in many deaths. One of the men injured in the Brick Lane bomb was walking along the street when he witnessed car doors flying into the air like paper. A four-inch shard of glass hit him in the head and he fell to the ground, only to awake in a pool of blood with people running scared in all directions.

London was suddenly on edge, as the second bomb had confirmed it was not a standalone incident. Police put various communities on alert and told the public to be suspicious of anything that seemed out of place, and not to approach any bag left in the street.

On Thursday 29th April, police released CCTV footage from the Brixton bombing of a man they believed was the suspect behind the attacks. He was seen dropping the bag then walking away. The press release came with an unusual warning that gay bars could be the next intended locations of an attack. Despite the race-hate links to the

Brixton and Brick Lane bombings, investigators were adamant that the gay community would be next – and they were right.

The release of the photo caused the bomber to bring the date of his attack forward by one day to Friday 30th April. 90 minutes before the final attack, an anonymous man called the police and claimed to have recognised the man in the footage as a former colleague of his, David Copeland. Police rushed to find out where Copeland was and what he was intending to do but it was too late.

The Admiral Duncan Pub in Old Compton Street, Soho, was packed as it was a Friday evening and the beginning of a long bank holiday weekend. People were outside on the street drinking and crowds were sandwiched into the pub. At 6.37pm, the heart of London's gay community was ripped apart by a massive explosion.

Admiral Duncan

Just a few minutes before the explosion, Copeland had walked into the pub and dropped a sports bag near to the bar. Some of the patrons noticed the bag and informed the manager. As the manager went to investigate the bag, the bomb was detonated.

The Admiral Duncan was ripped apart with the force of the explosion, and 1,500 four-inch nails were sent flying into patrons and people walking past the pub. Three people were killed in the attack, Andrea Dykes, 27, John Light, 32, and Nick Moore, 31. Andrea had recently been married, and her husband was injured in the bombing.

79 people were severely injured, with four of them needing to have limbs amputated. One of the patrons who was near the bag at the time, Jonathan Cash, remembered touching the bag with his foot as he was ordering a drink. He thought to himself that it might have been a bomb but believed those type of things happened to other people.

He was holding his drink in his hand when the bomb exploded. The table next to him had completely vanished and the next thing he knew, he was on his hands and knees on the street outside the bar. He found himself staring into a shop window, unable to recognise himself due to the bomb debris and injuries he had sustained.

Shockingly, he noticed a girl in her twenties exit a nearby pub with a pint of beer in her hand. She was apparently shouting homophobic slurs towards the destroyed Admiral Duncan and was overheard saying that she wanted to get a better view of the injured. The woman has never been identified, which was probably best, for her own safety at the time.

Fear rising

Another man close to ground zero, was Royal Mail worker Scott Terry who was inside the pub when the bomb exploded. He was thrown from the pub and landed on the street outside, with some parts of his body on fire. He was smothered by rescuers but he was also covered in blood, as 74 nails were embedded into his body.

Due to his injuries, sections of nine nails still remain embedded close to his spine to this day, as they are too dangerous to remove, with the fear they could cause massive nerve damage. Terry was induced into a coma for half-a-year. Many survivors of the bombings were left with not only physical scars but psychological ones too, with some developing severe mental health issues.

Two hours after the explosion, police received a phone call from the neo-Nazi White Wolves organisation who claimed responsibility for the attack. The White Wolves were linked to Combat 18 and were a group of white supremacists who once issued a blueprint of terror for attacks across London. By that time, police already knew Copeland was the suspect and were hunting him down.

Before they found him, the fear of attacks across London was getting worse. Many Jews, Chinese, and Irish communities shut down some of their businesses that night, with others stepping up security. It was suspected that synagogues might have been the location of the next attacks.

In the early hours of the following morning, police raided a house in the village of Cove, Hampshire, home to various rented rooms. One of the doors to a rented room opened and 22-year-old Copeland immediately told police he had carried out the three attacks.

He said, '*Yeah, they were all down to me. I did them on my own.*' He even invited police into the room, where he showed them the wall beside his bed. Two Nazi flags were hanging on the wall, along with a collection of photographs and newspaper cutting about the bombings. He was arrested and taken into custody.

Mr. Angry

As the city of London recovered from the bombings, Copeland was charged with three counts of murder and three counts of causing an explosion in order to endanger life. Now they had the nail bomber in custody, the police searched for the reasons behind the attacks, and uncovered a veil of hatred, racism, and sadomasochism.

Copeland was born in 1976 to a working-class couple in the London Borough of Hanworth. By the time he was 12, Copeland feared he was homosexual because he believed his parents were subliminally sending him messages telling him to be gay. When he was a teenager, he began having dreams about keeping women as slaves.

His dreams turned into fantasies, and he began to believe he had been reincarnated as an SS officer, whose job was to turn women into slaves and use them any way he wanted.

He left school and fell into various dead-end jobs, eventually blaming foreigners for taking the better jobs around him.

Weirdly, the teachers at his school have no real recollection of him, which meant he was simply floating through unseen, withdrawn from social interactions.

In his late teens, he became involved in petty crime such as minor theft and began drinking heavily and taking drugs. His withdrawal from society, combined with a growing hatred of foreigners and the gay community, led to him earning the nickname 'Mr. Angry.'

At the age of 21, in 1997, and with a hatred of the world growing within him, Copeland joined the British National Party (BNP). He became a steward at BNP meetings and became close with some of the more extreme members.

At around the same time, he downloaded the 'Terrorist's Handbook' from the burgeoning internet and learned how to make a bomb.

Set fire to the country

He left the BNP a year later, annoyed that the party wouldn't take part in direct paramilitary action. He joined the National Socialist Movement, a British neo-Nazi group active during the late 1990s. A few weeks before the bombings, Copeland began to suffer from mental delusions, and so he visited his GP, telling him that he was losing his mind and grip on reality.

The doctor simply prescribed him with anti-depressants and sent him on his way, believing that mental health intervention was not necessary. If mental health services had intervened at that time, then lives could have been saved.

In interviews with police, Copeland spoke of his neo-Nazi views and that he had worked alone. He wanted to set fire to the country and stir up a racial war, believing that there would be a backlash from ethnic minorities causing white people to go to war with them. His aim was to spread fear, resentment, and hatred, under the belief of a master race of white people.

Copeland's original target was going to be the Notting Hill Carnival but he decided on markets as he didn't have to wait a year for the carnival to come around. Copeland was sent to Broadmoor Hospital where he was diagnosed with having paranoid schizophrenia by five psychiatrists. When he went to court, the plea of guilty to manslaughter on the grounds of diminished responsibility was thrown out by the prosecution, and he was tried for murder.

On 30th June 2000, Copeland was found guilty of three counts of murder and three counts of causing an explosion in order to endanger life and was given six life sentences. In 2007, an order from the High Court was made to keep him in prison for at least fifty years. He is currently due for release in 2049, aged 73, but will likely spend the rest of his life behind bars.

The Ice Cream Wars

In 1980s Glasgow, rival criminal gangs were using ice cream vans to sell drugs and stolen goods, leading to the mass murder of six people and a man gluing himself to the railings of Buckingham Palace.

The Ice Cream Wars in Glasgow during the early 1980s resulted in mass murder, a 20-year long court case and bizarre behaviour from some of the people involved. It was one of the strangest yet most violent periods of Glasgow's history and was no place or time to be peddling ice cream.

From the 1960s in Glasgow, large housing projects were built, including the infamous Red Road site. Many of the sprawling council blocks had no additional development on them, which meant no supermarkets or other shops. This forced people to travel out of the developments to get what they needed.

To fulfil the need of the residents, ice cream van owners began repurposing their vehicles to sell groceries, including all the basics, along with newspapers and toilet paper. Very few at the time were actually selling ice creams.

The idea was that instead of having residents travel to a supermarket, the ice cream vans could come to them, negating the need for leaving the blocks. Some of the van owners were making a reasonable living but quickly discovered that if they sold contraband like cigarettes from abroad or stolen alcohol then they could make even more money.

Some of the vans decided that alongside selling Cornetto's and Magnums, they could bring in even more money by selling illegal drugs. This caught the attention of some of Glasgow's gangs in the early 1980s, who were looking for an easy way into some of the developments, as they were profitable locations to be in control of.

Serious Chimes Squad

As the gangs began infiltrating the ice cream vans, the once happy jingles coming out of the van's speakers meant that drugs were on the way into the estates. Soon, a battle began for control of the estates and that meant whoever owned or utilised the most ice cream vans was going to be bringing in the most profits.

Soon enough, Glasgow's Serious Crimes Squad, who were referred to as the Serious Chimes

Squad, began to cotton on that the vans were being used to smuggle drugs in and out of the estates. And soon enough, the Ice Cream Wars were in full effect.

Stories began emerging of ice cream van drivers attacking other vans with bricks and planks of wood, hoping to end the other's business. Many drivers, some of whom were not involved, began storing knives and axes in their vans out of fear of being attacked or accosted by the gangs.

With the knowledge that some ice cream vans carried drugs and other contraband, petty criminals began attacking vans to loot them. If they just so happened to attack a van that was run by one of the larger gangs, then the gangs retaliated with violence.

In the early 1980s, industry in Glasgow was collapsing at an unprecedented rate, leaving mass unemployment in the city. This led to public unrest and massive poverty, not helped by the sprawling estates gifted to them from the 1960s. Then, in 1984, the Ice Cream Wars came to a head when six people were murdered in an arson attack.

Mass murder

An 18-year-old ice cream van driver named Andrew Doyle was merely trying to keep his family above the poverty line by selling ice creams and other home goods. Despite being shot at while in his van one day, he had refused all the gang's advances to peddle drugs through his business.

He was warned by one of the gangs that he didn't have permission to operate on the housing estates but he ignored the warnings, which made him enemies. He was intimidated, threatened, shot at, and assaulted but still refused to stand down.

At around 2am on 16th April 1984, the gangs decided to frighten Doyle into working for them and targeted his Ruchazie property for an arson attack. The door of the property was doused in petrol and set alight. There were nine people staying in the property that night, and the resulting blaze killed six members of the Doyle family, including Andrew.

The six victims were James Doyle, 53, his daughter Christina Halleron, 25, her 18-month-old son Mark, and three of James' sons, James Jr., 23, Tony, 14, and Andrew. The mass murder shocked Scotland and the public quickly learned of the ice cream wars that were taking place in the country's largest city.

The police, who were already seen as inept in the eyes of the public, came under scrutiny as having failed to control gang violence in the city. Under pressure to bring justice to the Doyle family and Scotland, the police arrested many people in the months that followed including two men who spent 20 years proclaiming their innocence.

A witness, a statement, and a map of Glasgow

Four people were tried and convicted of offences relating to the ice cream wars. Two more, Thomas Campbell and Joe Steele were charged with the arson attack, convicted of murder, and sentenced to life in prison, with the judge handing down an order of a 20-year minimum term. Campbell was also convicted of the shooting of Doyle's van and given an additional 10 years.

What followed was a 20-year long court battle that involved hunger strikes, prison breakouts, political pandering, solitary isolation, prison beatings, appeals, and a belief that the police had ended up arresting two innocent men.

The case against Campbell and Steele rested on three main pieces of evidence, a witness, a statement, and a map of Glasgow with an X where Doyle's house was. The witness, William Love, claimed that he had overheard Campbell and Steele talking about arson while drinking in a city centre bar, and stated that they wanted to teach Doyle a lesson.

The police stated that Campbell had made a statement in which he said, '*I only wanted the van shot up. The fire at Fat Boy's was only meant to be a frightener which went too far.*'

The photocopied map of Glasgow with an X where Doyle's house sat, was found in Campbell's flat following his arrest.

Campbell was known to have been involved in the ice cream wars since 1983 and was keen to protect his patch against rival gang members. He was known as an enforcer, and Steele was his sidekick, recruited by Campbell for his campaign against rival gangs.

Both men claimed they had been set up by the witness, William Love, as he worked for a rival gang in secret, and that the evidence against them was falsified by police, including the map found in Campbell's flat.

Glued to Buckingham Palace

Campbell denied he had given a statement to police and that it had been constructed by them with the sole purpose of convicting someone for the Doyle murders. An appeal in 1989, five years after their conviction, failed to overturn their sentences.

In 1992, two journalists, Douglas Skelton and Lisa Brownlie, wrote a book about the ice cream wars entitled *Frightener*. In it, they interviewed William Love, who told them he had lied under oath for the simple reason that it suited his own selfish purposes and that the police pressured him to give evidence against Campbell.

What followed were a succession of failed appeals and Steele going to great lengths to prove his innocence. He went on a hunger strike several times and let his hair grow long. While he was allowed to visit his mother, he eloped from the prison officers, who later found him on a roof with banners claiming he was innocent.

Steele escaped from prison twice more, with the third and final time coming when he and four other inmates slipped through a wire fence during an outdoor exercise period. Steele travelled all the way to London to make a high-profile demonstration.

He made his way to Buckingham Palace where he superglued himself to the railings outside of the building. His plight made national news, and in some respects, the unusual demonstration brought massive public attention to his plight.

While he was glued to the railings, he told a journalist, *'if I had murdered the Doyle's, I would have admitted it and done my time quietly and without any fuss, to get an early release. I cannot admit guilt or show remorse for something I didn't do.'*

City of culture

The Buckingham Palace incident caused the British Secretary of State to refer the case to the appeal court. But the three judges reached a split decision which sent Campbell and Steele back to prison. After many more appeals, the pair's lawyers referred the case to the Scottish Criminal Cases Review Commission.

Three years later, in 2004, a new appeal court overturned the convictions, mostly on the basis of the flawed witness account from William Love and what the appeal court called significant misdirection of the jury. It was also concluded that Campbell's fake statement had been created by police in error, though many now see it as being constructed purely for the purpose of securing a conviction. In essence, the court of appeal decided the jury in the original trial was wrong.

Campbell and Steele walked out of court as free men in 2004, 20 years after the Doyle arson attack. Campbell and Steele later accused Glasgow gang boss Tam McGraw, who died in 2007, of being behind the arson attack, and that Tam had instigated a 20-year long campaign to keep them behind bars.

No new investigation into the Doyle murders was opened and the crime remains a stain on Glasgow's history. Glasgow has long since changed its image, having held the Commonwealth Games and the title of European City of Culture. But for some residents, they'll never forget the time that ice cream vans were peddling drugs within the city limits.

The Pendle Witches

In the summer of 1612, ten witches, six from two rival families, were found guilty of murder and witchcraft and executed at Gallows Hill, in one of the best-recorded witch trials in history.

Lancaster has a long and dark history and wasn't granted city status until 1937, its castle was still being used as a prison as recently as 2011. The city had a grim reputation for carrying out executions and is second only to London for the most people executed in England, giving it the unfortunate moniker of 'the hanging town'.

Perhaps the best known of the witch trials was the 17th Century trials of the Pendle witches, because in a rare move at the time, the entire trial and case were documented in a book titled, '*The Wonderfull Discoverie of Witches in the Countie of Lancaster.*' The spelling is as it was back then.

It was written by the clerk of the court, Thomas Potts, and due to its detailed account of the trials, the legend of the Pendle witches is not so much legend, but fact, at least, in relation to the trial itself. The notion that the 10 people executed from the trials were real witches depends very much where one stands on the spectrum of the occult or paranormal.

Bear in mind that in the 17th Century, the humble hedgehog was associated with witchcraft, with some people believing that a hedgehog was a witch in disguise and could shape-shift and venture into any building to cause harm to others. Though it should be noted that witches were associated with many small animals – demons sent out to do their bidding.

In 1612, the Pendle witch trials took place, in which 12 people were accused of witchcraft, who lived in and around the Pendle Hill region of Lancashire. In total, they were charged with the murders of ten people using the dark magic of witchcraft. One died in prison while awaiting trial, and of the 11 remaining witches, only one was found not guilty. The other 10 were executed by hanging.

Rival families

Six of the 11 witches on trial came from two rival families, the Demdike's and the Chattox's, who were overseen by two elderly widows. Elizabeth Southerns was known as Old Demdike and had been known as a witch for over 50 years, which makes it surprising that she wasn't executed sooner.

However, in the 16th to 17th Centuries in England, it was a mostly accepted part of village life that there was a healer in the village who practiced unorthodox magic and sold herbs and medicines. Witchcraft was made a capital offence in Britain in 1563, but Pope Innocent VIII had deemed it heresy since 1484.

From 1484 to the 1750's, over 200,000 witches were tortured, burned alive, or executed in Western Europe. It might be surprising to learn that only 500 of those took place in England, 1,500 in Scotland, and only five in Wales.

Old Demdike's rival was Anne Whittle, known as Mother Chattox, and they fought with each other over business in the village, as both families were offering similar services. In fact, many of the accusations of witchcraft came from members of both families, as they sought to stop the competition, so, in some way, the trials were caused by themselves.

The event that led to the Pendle witch trials took place on 21st March 1612, when Old Demdike's granddaughter, Alizon Device, was out walking in Trawden Forest. She approached a street seller named John Law, and asked him for some pins, which were sometimes used in witchcraft to treat a variety of ailments.

Law refused to sell her the pins and carried on his way but a few moments later, he collapsed. Alizon watched as he managed to get back to his feet and stumble into a local Inn. She believed she had caused the man to fall down with her powers and thought she was more powerful than she first realised. Though, in reality, John Law may have suffered a mild stroke.

Bickering of witches

John's son accosted Alizon a couple of days later and took her to see his father. While there, believing she had used her powers to make him fall down, she confessed to hurting him using witchcraft and begged for forgiveness. As word got around that Old Demdike's granddaughter had used witchcraft on another person, the story caught the attention of Roger Nowell, who was the justice of the peace for Pendle – a judicial officer of a lower court.

Alizon, her brother James, and their mother Elizabeth Device were summoned by Nowell to appear in court on 30th March. There, Alizon confessed she had sold her soul to the Devil and used her connection with the dark lord to make John Law fall to the ground. Elizabeth confessed that her mother, Old Demdike, had a mark on her body that was left by the Devil sucking her blood.

Alizon quickly realised that instead of giving up her entire family, she could also get the Chattox family charged with witchcraft – and an opportunity for revenge. In the ten years prior to the John Law incident, members of the Chattox family had stolen goods from Device's home and caused damage to their property. Alizon also accused the family of killing five men, including her own father who died in 1601.

She claimed that her father was so scared of Mother Chattox that he agreed to give her a bag of oatmeal each year in return for leaving his family alone. In 1601, he forgot to hand over the oatmeal and became ill. On his deathbed, he blamed Mother Chattox for his illness, which eventually killed him.

On 2nd April 1612, Old Demdike and Mother Chattox were taken from their home and appeared in court, along with Chattox's daughter, Anne Redferne. Both matriarchs were blind and in their eighties, a noble age in the 17th Century. Both women confessed to selling their souls to the devil but that the other was responsible for deaths in the region.

The following day, after hearing all the evidence and statements, Nowell and the judge detained Alizon, Anne, Old Demdike and Mother Chattox and set a date for trial.

While awaiting trial, Old Demdike died in the dungeons of Lancaster Castle, unable to live with the dark, damp conditions.

My mother is a witch

Before the trial, James Device, Alizon's brother, stole a neighbours sheep which caused Nowell to investigate the family further. Eight more people were committed to the same trial, including Elizabeth Device, James Device, Alice Nutter, Katherine Hewitt, Jane Bulcock and her son John, Alice Grey and Jennet Preston, who had all met at Malkin Tower to allegedly plan various murders.

Preston was sent to trial in York as she lived in Yorkshire, and the other seven were sent to Lancaster prison to join the other three. Preston's trial took place first in York on 27th July 1612. It materialised that she had met James Device to plan the murder of a Thomas Lister, a local landowner close to York, who Preston had fought with for years.

When she was taken to see Lister's body, it was said that the corpse bled fresh blood from its orifices. Preston was executed two days later by hanging, the first of ten executions.

The pendle witch trials took place between 17th and 19th August 1612, and ultimately rested on the evidence given by nine-year-old Jennet Device, who was allowed to testify as witch trials fell under different rules than other trials. She identified all the people who had attended the murder meeting at Malkin Tower and gave evidence against her own mother, Elizabeth.

'My mother is a witch and that I know to be true. I have seen her spirit in the likeness of a brown dog, which she calls Ball. The dog did ask what she would have him do, and she answered that she would have him help her to kill.' – Jennet Device

When Elizabeth heard her daughter testify against her, she had to be physically removed from the court as she was screaming and cursing at her daughter with a maniacal look on her face. Modern investigators posit that Jennet was coerced to testify but it has never been proven.

City of witches

Alice Grey was the only person in the trial who was found not guilty. She was accused alongside Katherine Hewitt of murdering Anne Foulds the year before. Alice was said to have been at the meeting at Malkin Tower but was not deemed to be involved in any witchcraft and was ultimately acquitted. Katherine was found guilty and sentenced to death and was linked with a child murder a few years earlier.

Mother Chattox was found guilty of the murder of Robert Nutter, after a former house guest, James Robinson, accused Chattox of turning his beer sour and witnessed her take part in dark magic. Upon his testimony, Anne broke down and confessed she had sold her soul to the Devil.

James Device was found guilty of the murders of villagers Anne Townley and John Duckworth, after his nine-year-old sister Jennet confessed she had seen James talking with a black dog to help him conjure up a spell to kill Townley.

Anne Redferne was found guilty of the murder of Robert Nutter's father, Christopher, after various witnesses came forward to claim that Anne was a far more dangerous witch than her mother, Old Demdike.

Jane Bulcock and her son were found guilty of witchcraft and the murder of Jennet Deane purely on the basis of testimony from Jennet Device, who identified them as being at the meeting. Alice Nutter was found guilty of the murder of Henry Mitton, despite not confessing or having no evidence against her aside from Jennet Device's identification of her.

When John Law was brought in as a witness in the case of Alizon Device, Alizon saw him and immediately fell to her knees to beg for forgiveness, confessing her sins upon the world. She was the only person on trial who truly believed she had the power of a witch.

On 20th August 1612, Alizon, Elizabeth, and James Device, Anne Redferne, Alice Nutter, Katherine Hewitt, John and Jane Bulcock, and Mother Chattox were led to an open field and hanged at Gallows Hill in Lancaster.

The Pendle witch trials are one of the most recorded witch trials in history and shows just how far the establishment went to rid witches from the land. It's an unusual story, in that most of the accusations and evidence came from members of the same family, rival families, and friends. If they hadn't accused each other of witchcraft then the trials may not have ever taken place.

In Lancaster today, over 400 years later, the Pendle witches remain a big draw to the city and are responsible for increased tourism to the area. The city is home to the Pendle Witch Trail which leads to Lancaster Castle, a local bus called The Witch Way, a beer called the Pendle Witches Brew, and an annual Halloween gathering on Gallows Hill, where the witches were executed.

The Playboy Bunny and the Schoolgirl Murders

A Playboy Bunny and a schoolgirl were attacked and killed in two separate incidents in London six months apart, by the same killer who has never been identified.

Two murders in 1975, six months apart, were connected 30 years later by DNA evidence. London Playboy Bunny, Eve Stratford, was killed in Leyton on 18th March, and schoolgirl Lynne Weedon was killed six months later on 3rd September. Both murders remain unsolved and have haunted their respective families and cold case investigators to this day.

Eve was born in Dortmund, Germany, in 1953 to a German mother and English soldier, and she went on to win various beauty contests in the area in her childhood and early teen years. After travelling around the world with their jobs, the family finally settled on Aldershot in Hampshire in 1972, when Eve was 18.

In the same year, Eve hooked up with Tony Priest, who was the lead singer of English psychedelic rock band Onyx, who were active from 1965 to 1971. They quickly became close and Eve moved into a flat with him and two other band members in Leyton, North London.

In 1973, when she was 19, Eve became a waitress at the Playboy Club in Mayfair, which exists to this day. She had big ambitions of becoming a model and would aim to achieve that goal by using any means necessary. She quickly became a regular at the club and was known to be the favourite of the club owners, who paraded her around to attract customers.

Photos exist of Eve mingling with the likes of comedians Eric Morecambe and Sid James, and boxing legend John Conteh. Eve was so intent on becoming a model that she fought hard to feature in Playboy's American magazine. When she was turned down, she managed to be featured in the British rival to Playboy, an adult magazine called Mayfair.

Under the stage name of Eva Von Borke, she posed topless on the front cover as Miss March for the Spring Bonanza issue in 1975. She was pictured across nine pages with full frontal nudes, in an edition that sold almost half a million copies.

Due to appearing in Mayfair, the boss of the Playboy club suspended her for three months but it was suspected her killer had already selected Eve as a victim due to her appearance in the magazine. She would be killed just days after the magazine hit the shelves.

Bunny murder

The boss of the Playboy club claimed that Eve was happy with the suspension as she believed the Mayfair spread was the stepping-stone to a greater modelling career. He was reported as saying that '*she wanted to do something with her life, and not wait on tables forever.*'

After posing for Mayfair, Eve took part in two more photoshoots, one for a South African pornographic magazine and another as a model for a crime novel, in which she was displayed semi-nude with a knife pressed against her throat, in a grim foreshadowing of what was to come.

On Tuesday 17th March 1975, just days after Mayfair hit the shelves of every newsagent in the country, Eve left her agent's office to walk home to her apartment. She arrived at around 4pm and was heard talking to an unidentified man by a neighbour.

The same neighbour heard a thud 30 minutes later as if something or someone had been thrown to the floor followed shortly after by footsteps coming down the stairs and out of the property. The neighbour never saw who it was. Approximately 15 minutes later, Eve's boyfriend, Tony, and one of his bandmates, arrived home to a bloody crime scene. Eve had been tied up at her wrists and ankles and viciously raped. She had been stabbed in the neck 12 times, with the wounds being so severe they had almost decapitated her.

A bunch of flowers she had brought herself on the way home were found in the hallway of the flat. In less than 30 minutes, an unidentified man had raped and killed the ambitious model, leaving a crime scene that shocked London. Six months later, the same killer struck again, this time raping and killing a 16-year-old schoolgirl.

The schoolgirl

On Wednesday 3rd September, 16-year-old schoolgirl Lynne Weedon went on a night out with friends to celebrate their school exam results in Hounslow. They stayed in the local Elm Tree pub for most of the night until last orders were called.

Just after 11pm, Lynne started the ten minute walk home alone but someone had followed her from the pub. As she turned into an alleyway known as The Short Hedges, she was hit in the back of the head and fell to the ground. The attacker lifted her up over a high fence and threw her into an electricity substation.

Lynne was dragged away from the fence, raped, and beaten with a heavy blunt instrument which was never recovered but thought to have been a lead pipe. The alleyway, close to the local school, was notorious for people hanging around after dark but no murder had ever taken place there until Lynne's. The following morning, the caretaker of the school, whose house overlooked the substation, looked out his window and saw Lynne's body on the ground. Despite her horrific injuries, which included having a fractured skull, Lynne was alive when emergency services arrived at the scene.

Unfortunately, she never regained consciousness and died in hospital a week later on 10th September, which led to a murder enquiry being opened. Two witnesses claimed to have seen a white man running away from the scene at around the time of the murder but it was too dark to make an identification.

Eve's investigation

At around the time of Lynne's murder, Eve's murder was still being investigated. Police concluded that the Mayfair spread had tempted her killer because the attack was sexual in nature and due to the magazine being released a few days before her death. The apartment had not been broken into and the neighbours heard no shouting or screaming, which suggested that Eve knew her attacker. In 1970s London, tracking someone's postal address would have been easy, privacy laws were very different back then.

In the Mayfair spread, Eve spoke of her bisexuality and how she liked being dominated sexually by men and how she enjoyed playing games with her lovers. She also said she lived alone with her cat, which wasn't true as she lived in the flat with her boyfriend and his bandmates.

The nude photos, the preference of being dominated, the statement of living alone, a known club where people could see her work, all led to Eve being selected as a victim. The flowers found in the hallway suggested that her killer had either followed her home or was waiting near to the entrance and accosted her by the front door.

It's possible that Eve knew her attacker as a customer at the Playboy club or maybe she was overpowered as soon as the front door opened. It seems more than likely that she was overpowered due to the flowers on the floor.

Other workers at the Playboy club were interviewed and one of them claimed she had received death threats by phone after she appeared in a similar adult magazine. Eve was also known to have received mysterious phone calls where the caller would simply breathe on the other end and not talk.

In October 1975, a landlord was cleaning out a flat in Liverpool after it had been vacated by two male tenants when he found something suspicious and called police. Newspaper reports of Eve's murder were nailed to the wall with darts and smeared with lipstick, and many pictures of her had been stabbed with the darts. A year later, the investigation into Eve's murder ended, as police had exhausted all leads and had no evidence to go on. But the brutality of the crime would not go unnoticed and it would be another 30 years before her murder was linked with Lynne's.

An unusual killer

Eve and Lynne's killer – or killers – would have been very strong. It would take a lot of strength to drag a grown woman up the stairs to her apartment and the same amount of strength to lift a 16-year-old girl over a high fence and throw her to the ground on the other side.

The killer slashed and stabbed Eve in the neck 12 times which almost caused a decapitation, which again would have needed considerable strength, it also would have been pre-planned, as Eve was killed after she was raped, most likely to stop the killer being identified.

Lynne was hit over the head with a heavy object, instead of being stabbed, and she would have been unconscious when she was raped. The killer then hit her again before leaving and assumed she would have died, but she wouldn't have been able to identify him as she was first hit from behind.

In 2004, cold case investigators reopened Lynne's case and looked at all the details but came up with nothing new. Then in 2007, due to advancements in DNA technology, investigators were shocked to discover that the same killer was responsible for both Lynne's and Eve's murders.

Which was unusual due to the manner in which they were killed and the different type of victims they were, one being an adult model and the other a local schoolgirl. The DNA didn't match anyone on the databases, and genealogy testing has proved fruitless.

A dark secret

A profile of the killer was drawn up and suggested he was a white male between the ages of 17 to 30 and may not have committed any crime beyond 1995, when DNA began to be collected from those alleged with committing crime.

Many psychiatrists and profilers have looked at both murders and claimed it would be unusual if the killer did not ever confess to anyone, and almost impossible to have kept a dark secret such as murder for so long. He was also thought to be someone local to Hounslow, due to his knowledge of the alleyway that Lynne took on that fateful night.

Both rapes and murders were premeditated and it seemed unlikely that the killer only claimed two victims. If he had killed again then he may have developed new methods to hide his victim's bodies or claimed a victim that has not yet been linked to him.

The possibilities relating to the two cases are endless. It's possible there was an error in the DNA testing, which has happened before, resulting in a contaminated test accidentally linking two bodies where there was no link. However, the DNA has been tested again for good measure and there is a match.

There could have been two killers, which would explain the strength needed to lift the victims, and maybe they both raped the victims with one taking extra precautions to not leave any evidence, but it seems unlikely as multiple rape/murders are rarely committed in pairs.

Despite the DNA evidence, some researchers and authors have pointed to the killer as Peter Sutcliffe but the DNA evidence does indeed rule him out. There is also the belief that Eve's murder was covered up as it may have been someone famous and well-known from the Playboy club but again it wouldn't explain why Lynne was murdered, unless to go all-in on the cover-up story.

There are a large number of cold cases in the UK but none quite as baffling as the murders of the Playboy Bunny and the schoolgirl. It appears that without new evidence, both cases will forever remain unsolved, and the killer will have got away with at least two murders.

The Wardell Murder

After a body of a woman was found near a motorway, police rushed to her home to find her husband bound and gagged, claiming they were attacked by a man in a clown mask – but a twist this way comes.

Born in 1955 Coventry, Carol Heslop had a passion for ten-pin bowling and went on to become a member of the Coventry bowling league, where she met her future husband, Gordon Wardell in 1979. They married three years later, and Carol took a job as a cashier at the Coventry branch of the Woolwich Building Society, a financial institution bought out by Barclays in 2000.

She was so good at her job that she quickly rose the ranks, and by 1992 was promoted to branch manager at the nearby Nuneaton branch, nine miles north. By that time, the loving couple were living in the village of Meriden, seven miles from Coventry and only 16 from Birmingham.

As far as family and friends could tell, the relationship between Carol and Gordon was moving smoothly and the pair were seen as relatively wealthy. Gordon had climbed the ranks of a car component business to the point where he was an executive manager but he was taking a lot of time off work.

While Carol was out working, Gordon lived a secret lifestyle where he became addicted to using sex workers. He paid £50 each time to various women to have sex with him while he was tied up, something which he had grown to enjoy.

Six months before her murder, 39-year-old Carol had found out about 42-year-old Gordon's fetish for sex workers and refused to have sex with him. It was about the same time that Gordon was fired from his job for reasons that have never been disclosed, probably due to the amount of time he was taking off.

Then, in September 1994, murder found its way to Nuneaton. In the early morning of the 21st, Carol's lifeless body was spotted by a passing motorist at the side of a grassy verge on the A444, a country road in the Nuneaton area. It sparked a murder investigation unlike any seen in the area before.

Robbery

Detectives arrived on the scene quickly and cordoned off the area. Carol had been strangled to death and there had been no attempt to hide the body, her left sandal was found metres away but her right one was missing. It was suspected she was thrown from a moving vehicle.

Half hour later, staff members from the Nuneaton branch of The Woolwich phoned police to report a break-in, and that there was no sign of their boss, Carol, who was the key-owner for the building. Suspecting an armed robbery, the police sent in the big guns.

Armed police arrived at the scene along with a helicopter that remained stationary above the building. They entered the branch and found there was no sign of forced entry, the alarms hadn't gone off, but all the cash from the vault was missing.

The detectives at the murder scene learned from forensic officers that Carol's own security code had been used to access the vault at approximately 5am that morning, and that her own keys were used to unlock the main door.

Just over £14,000 and numerous blank cheques were missing from the vault. This, along with Carol's body led detectives to the logical conclusion that Carol had been kidnapped and used by armed robbers to access the vault, before being murdered and dumped on the side of the road.

But by that point, no one had heard from Gordon Wardell. There might have been a slim possibility that the armed robbers were in the Wardell's property holding Gordon hostage, so armed police and the detectives descended on the home.

Police forced their way into the property, expecting to find either a dead body or resistance from armed robbers. Instead, what met them was an unusual sight. Gordon was found in his underwear, gagged, and tied to a chair in the middle of the front room.

A clown mask

His clothes were folded neatly beside him, and he appeared to be in a state of distress. He had been gagged with a strip of cloth and tied to a refuse sack holder with two ratchet ties around his wrists. Despite being conscious and alert, he was found with bruising on his stomach and chest.

Paramedics arrived on the scene but didn't have to do much as Gordon's bruises were superficial and didn't require care, they also noted that his blood pressure and heartbeat were low, which would have been odd considering the ordeal that Gordon claimed he went through.

He stated that he arrived home from the pub at 10pm the night before, to find a man wearing a clown mask and boiler suit and holding his wife at knifepoint on the living room sofa. Two other men grabbed him from behind and used some kind of chemical to knock him out for at least ten hours.

Gordon became conscious at around 6am but couldn't escape from his restraints to alert police, which they found unusual as the ratchet ties around his wrists were noted as being '*loose enough to have escaped from with ease, should one have wanted to.*'

For a little while longer, detectives believed his story but the following day, while he was being interviewed by them, his story began to break down. It appeared that there might not have been a kidnapping at all and that Gordon was behind the robbery and his wife's murder.

Previous attack

Despite their suspicions, detectives decided to hold a press conference, not least as it was part of the murder process when a suspect had not been arrested, but also to see how Gordon would cope with different questions being put to him.

Regardless of his superficial wounds, Gordon appeared at the press conference in a wheelchair, wearing sunglasses, and acting nervously around people. Through tears, he told the same story to the press, that a man in a clown mask held his wife at knifepoint, before he was rendered unconscious by two other men.

He then claimed not to have remembered anything else until he awoke later bound and gagged in the front room and was frantically trying to get help even though he couldn't escape his loose ties. One reporter asked him about a previous conviction for assault and attempted rape but he waved off the question as not being relevant to the press conference. Except, it was.

Gordon was known to police in the area for a horrific attack he had carried out in the 1970s when he was only 17. He had attacked the wife of his school's science teacher with a knife and sexually assaulted her. The teacher went on to survive the attack and Gordon served four years in jail for the crime.

It was a worrying sign to the detectives that Gordon may have been involved in his own wife's murder but they had no real evidence to go on so they set up a crime scene reconstruction to have Gordon go over his story multiple times.

Holes in the story

On 2nd October, the police carried out a reconstruction of his movements, with Gordon alongside them. He retraced his steps of posting some letters in the early evening before going to The Brooklands pub on the outskirts of Coventry, having two drinks then driving home – where he found his wife being held at knifepoint.

The reconstruction was covered by local and national press, in the hopes that someone may come forward with more information but no one did, which was unusual, as Gordon had visited very public places but no one claimed to have seen him.

Staff and customers at The Brooklands had no recollection of Gordon drinking there that night, despite him being seen there on previous nights. There was also no evidence that suggested he had posted letters.

A day after the reconstruction, two Coventry-based sex workers went to police and said they recognised Gordon from numerous encounters between them, and that he preferred being tied up, along with 'kinky sex'. By that point, police were already suspicious of Gordon due to numerous reasons, not least his story.

The way that Gordon described his own attack didn't make sense. Gordon claimed that two men had come at him from both sides as he entered through the front door but there would not have been space for two men to be hiding.

Forensic experts found no trace of any chemical used to knock him out, nor was there any chemical delivered in that manner that could render a man unconscious in a few seconds and last for ten hours, despite Gordon claiming it to be a chloroform-based drug.

There was only one clown that night

It was odd for his clothes to be folded up and placed next to him after he had been tied up. It also remained odd for his clothes to have been removed in the first place and wasn't something that would have been required to tie him up.

His restraints were loose and it was concluded that anyone could have worked their wrists out of it. The fact that they were ratchet ties and not something like rope or cord, made it easier for a person to tie themselves up. The gag could easily have been put on before he tied himself. His bruises were also inconsistent with his story and were superficial.

And then there was The Woolwich. All branch managers, including Carol, were given special codes to use if they were being forced to unlock the branch or vault. The codes would unlock everything as normal but send a distress call to police. Carol hadn't used the distress codes.

With the holes in the story, police arrested Gordon on 20th October 1994 on the suspicion of his wife's murder. With no other suspects in the mix, he was charged four days later. His trial was held in 1995, with the prosecution claiming he had executed an elaborate scheme to deceive police, divert attention away from himself, and get away with murder.

The six week trial involved 128 witnesses, including numerous sex workers who identified Gordon as one of their clients. He was convicted of murder and robbery, and four days before

Christmas in 1995, was sentenced to life in prison with a minimum tariff of 18 years.

An appeal was held in 2007, to reduce Gordon's sentence, but in the background, police had begun to link him to the murders of various sex workers around Coventry and Birmingham pre-1994 and fought to keep him in prison.

The judge at the appeal stated that Gordon would likely never be released and increased his life tariff to include an additional 18 years. Gordon still remains a suspect in the murders of at least two sex workers but has never been charged.

The murder of Carol Wardell and the resulting deception by Gordon is unlike any case seen in the area before or after. The only clown in the house that night was Gordon, who created the façade of a circus to ultimately get away with murder – which he didn't.

Britain's Youngest Serial Killer

A 15-year-old boy claiming he was possessed by the Devil and heard voices telling him to kill, stabbed to death two people and was caught while planning a third.

Colchester in 2014, was the location of two brutal murders carried out by a 15-year-old boy named James Fairweather. The crimes themselves are vicious enough but the fact he was still in high school makes the whole story just that little bit creepier.

Fairweather was born in 1998 in the market town of Colchester and attended high school at the Colchester Academy where he was known to be bullied for his larger than normal ears. He suffered from dyslexia and autism which wasn't diagnosed until after his arrest.

He was described as a normal boy who was quiet in school and was seen as having come from a good family. As he grew into his teenage years, he turned into an angry, hateful boy who wanted to go to war with the world around him. When asked what he wanted to be in the future, he stared at the teacher and said, '*a murderer*'.

His grandmother died of natural causes in 2012, when he was 13, and it was suggested her death had a larger impact on him that people around him realised. A year later, he was arrested of causing criminal damage to a house.

In January 2014, he was sentenced to a year's supervision which clearly didn't work. Only three days before the first murder, he was arrested again for the knifepoint robbery of cigars from another person but released without charge.

While he was supposed to have been supervised, he murdered two people in the most brutal of fashions. After his grandmother's death, Fairweather fell in love with serial killers and became obsessed with Peter Sutcliffe.

Bleeding into the grass

He claimed his favourite serial killer was Ted Bundy, which says a lot. A murder involves the death of a real-life person whose life was violently ended by another. To say that a serial killer can be a favourite, above other murderers, and bundled in with food, film, and games, is abhorrent.

And yet, Fairweather was affected by his love of Sutcliffe and Bundy so much that he sought to become like them. His murders caused the largest investigation ever carried out by Essex police. What makes this case rarer is that the press held off from releasing the details of the murders due to their ferocity and didn't name Fairweather until after the trial.

Fairweather's first victim was 33-year-old father of five James Attfield, who had gone out drinking on the night of March 29th 2014 and decided to lay down to rest in Castle Park. Attfield had previously suffered brain damage after a car crash and would often be seen out drinking in the town.

Just before midnight, Fairweather left his family home with a knife, purely with the intention of killing someone and claiming his first victim. As he traipsed through the park, he saw Attfield on the grass, and with no one else around, Fairweather selected him to kill.

He jumped on top of Attfield and stabbed him 102 times in his torso, face, and limbs, before walking away and arriving back home at around 2.30am. Just after 5.30am, a local man was walking through the park when he discovered the mangled body of Attfield, bleeding into the grass.

When paramedics arrived, they remarkably discovered a weak pulse but Attfield died of his wounds an hour later. When press got wind of the story, a decision was made not to release the details as they were too gruesome to describe. Fairweather later said that the voices in his head began to laugh as he stabbed Attfield to death.

Second bloody murder

Police cordoned off a 1.5 mile area around the park to search for evidence linking them to the madman. Detectives were drafted in from Kent police and the Essex Serious Crime Directorate, to investigate a murder that had shocked the country.

Police questioned 70 local people who had been associated with knife crime, including Fairweather but he convinced them of a false alibi and he wasn't questioned any further, with his mother, suspecting nothing, confirming his story. Police also assumed that someone who carried out such a vicious attack could not have been a 15-year-old boy.

An innocent man was arrested a week later but was released without charge due to a strong alibi. For the next three months, the police struggled to find any evidence strong enough to arrest another suspect but then the madman struck again.

In the middle of the day on June 17th, 31-year-old Saudi-Arabian student Nahid Almanea was walking along a nature trial to her University campus, when she was attacked. Fairweather stabbed her in the stomach 10 times, then as she fell, stabbed her in both eyes before shoving the knife into her brain, killing her instantly. He later claimed he stabbed her in the eyes so that she could not see evil.

Suddenly, within three months, Colchester had been subjected to two vicious, bloody murders, and the police were already at a loss. There was no connection between the two victims at all and it was first suspected that Almanea was the victim of a hate crime, leading police to believe they were looking for two killers.

In the following months as the murders went unsolved, many residents of Colchester refused to leave their homes or went out only in pairs or in large groups. The council cut down and cleared out a lot of the city's overgrown fields and walkways to reduce the number of hiding places the killer could be lurking – but it was a hiding place that would finally lead to Fairweather's arrest.

Hiding in the undergrowth

Fairweather later claimed that he didn't kill again because of the intense public interest in the case but was waiting for the right moment to strike again. Many residents of Colchester also believed the killer had come from outside the area.

On 27th May 2015, almost a year after the Almanea murder, Fairweather decided to kill again. At 11am that morning, a local woman was walking her dog along the Salary Brook nature trial when she spotted a hooded teenager hiding in the bushes wearing surgical gloves. She immediately turned around and called police who arrived at her location within minutes.

They closed in on Fairweather, who was 16 at that point, and pulled him from the undergrowth where he was hiding. When they searched him, they found a lock-knife and surgical gloves, which he was later confirmed to have worn at both murders to avoid fingerprint detection.

At the time of his capture, he had left the academy while studying for his GCSE's as he didn't think it was for him, and instead tried to find a job. All the other pupils at the school had no idea that a serial killer was sitting with them in class.

Fairweather admitted to the murders when interviewed by police and claimed that he was looking for a third victim that very morning. At his home, they found documentaries on Peter Sutcliffe and other serial killers, violent video games, and stashes of horror movies. It's important to note that true crime and horror is only bad to those who already have, like Fairweather, a disposition to violent thoughts.

A monster

In August 2015, before his trial, many psychiatrists spoke with him and later revealed shocking details. He claimed that he had fantasies of burning babies and maiming sex workers, and that the voices in his head told him to seek out victims.

When asked where the voices came from, he said that he had been possessed by the Devil but didn't exactly know when it had happened. He said that for some reason, he needed to kill 15 people to satisfy the Devil, and blamed Almanea's murder on the fact she was simply walking alone.

The trial began in January 2016 at the Old Bailey, the Central Criminal Court of England and Wales in Central London. Fairweather pleaded not guilty to two counts of murder but admitted to two charges of manslaughter on the grounds of diminished responsibility.

A court psychiatrist denied the fact that Fairweather had a mental health condition, instead diagnosing him with autism, meaning that Fairweather was deemed fit to stand trial. On 29th April 2016, the then 17-year-old Fairweather was sentenced to life in prison with a minimum term of 27 years. After hearing the sentence, Fairweather turned to his distraught parents and said, '*I don't give a shit.*'

The judge in the trial claimed that Fairweather was in full control of his actions and rejected the notion that his mental functions caused the murders, which he said would be an unjustified slur against autistic people. Fairweather's name was supposed to have been kept out of the press but the public pushed hard for the killer to be named.

After the trial, various psychiatrists interviewed Fairweather and claimed the court psychiatrist was wrong in that Fairweather was indeed suffering from severe psychosis. Some of the hallucinations that Fairweather was having made even the hardened psychiatrist sick to their stomach and were allegedly like something out of a horror story.

An appeal to reduce Fairweather's sentence in late 2016 failed when the judge confirmed he would remain in prison for the rest of his life, and if any parole board decided to release him, that he would remain on license forever.

For the families of the two victims, they still cannot fathom how such a young boy could kill in such a fashion. Attfield's mother labelled Fairweather as a monster, and as a result of her son's death could no longer work, which meant she lost her home. Almanea's brother claimed that their mother's tears have never dried and their father could not understand why she had been taken from them.

Fairweather is without doubt one of the most vicious killers to have ever lived in Essex, if not the country, made worse by his age and the failure of a system to keep him in check. He has since become infamous as Britain's youngest serial killer.

The Camden Ripper

A devil-worshipping serial killer brutally murdered and dismembered at least three sex workers before dumping their body parts in canals and bins around Camden.

Camden is nothing if not the epicentre of a world's worth of bonkers and varied lifestyles, I should know, I live there. As with many London boroughs, crime exists, sometimes obviously, other times not so much, but there is always the feeling that the nights are considered riskier than the day.

Beyond the world food stalls, crowds of visitors, alternative fashion, and labyrinthine markets, there exists a town that's earned its worth as one of London's most popular areas. But throw a serial killer into the mix, and Camden is pushed to the edge.

Born in 1951, Anthony John Hardy became known as the Camden Ripper, for the murders of three women in 2002. It was an unusual case, as his lifestyle and age didn't fit the profile the police had drawn up to catch him, as he claimed his first convicted victim when he was 51-years-old.

He grew up in Burton-upon-Trent in Staffordshire to a hard-working family and allegedly had a good childhood with no indication of what was to come. After earning good school grades, he enrolled at the illustrious Imperial College London where he graduated with a degree in engineering.

While studying for his degree, he met his future wife Judith Dwight, who he married in 1972. Over the next few years, Hardy became the manager of a large company and had three sons and one daughter with Judith.

Due to his work, he moved the family to Tasmania, Australia, where the children were raised. But from 1982, Hardy began to change, and there was no obvious moment when it happened. He was known to have displayed symptoms of mental illness but wasn't diagnosed with anything at the time.

In fact, Hardy's case sits very much in the nurture camp of the nurture vs. nature debate, in that he turned to the dark side in his thirties, finding a passion for devil worship and a kinship with none other than Jack the Ripper.

Descent into madness

While in Tasmania in 1982, Hardy attacked Judith. He filled a water bottle and froze it before using it to hit Judith over the head as she slept. He then dragged her unconscious body to the bathtub where he attempted to drown her. Fortunately, she awoke and managed to fight him off.

Judith didn't press charges but Hardy agreed to check himself into a psychiatric hospital in Queensland, where he stayed for a month before being placed under mental health care. Following on from that, he ended up stalking Judith for a couple of years and told a psychiatrist that he wanted to kill her.

In 1985, Hardy left his family in Australia and returned to the UK. In 1986, Judith was successful in obtaining a divorce from him because of the stalking and worrying behaviour. She also gained custody of their children and remained in Australia, which sent Hardy on a downward spiral.

Over the next few years, Hardy was in and out of psychiatric hospitals and mental health care and diagnosed with depression and bipolar disorder. He quickly turned to drink and drugs as a way to cope with his life.

When he was a child, he promised himself that he would escape his working class roots and become someone better than the life he was given. And for a while, being manager of a company and a growing family, he lived his promise. But the divorce left him on the bread line with no job and family, and so Hardy developed a hatred not only of himself, but the world around him.

He was admitted to various hospitals for alcohol abuse and was often found in a drug-induced psychosis, where he couldn't remember his own name. He lived in various hostels around London due to being homeless a lot of the time, before getting a council flat on a quiet Camden estate, at Number 4 Hartland, Royal College Street.

Body parts around London

Throughout the 1990s, and in his forties, he began using sex workers from money he had made selling on stolen goods. He was arrested multiple times for theft but got away with a prison term each time due to his deteriorating mental health.

In 1998, Hardy was arrested when a sex worker accused him of raping her. Police investigated the incident but concluded there was not enough evidence to charge Hardy, who yet again, was admitted to a psychiatric hospital.

Many of Hardy's neighbours later spoke of his strange behaviour and that he acted strange around other people and was argumentative, especially when it came to communal areas. He was once found in the bin area sitting on the floor, hitting a hammer on the ground for no apparent reason. He was also spotted going through neighbours bins and taking some of their rubbish back into his flat. What police didn't know at the time but were later made aware of was that Hardy was discharged from a London psychiatric hospital just days before he claimed his first victim. Though convicted of three murders, Hardy was positively linked to two more.

On 17th December 2000, a man walking along the River Thames near Battersea, spotted something unusual in the water at the side of the riverbank. He moved in for a closer look and realised it was the upper body of a female, who had been severed at the waist.

Medical examiners concluded she had been in the water for at least two weeks and had been sliced in half with a sword or machete. She was later identified through tattoo recognition as 24-year-old sex worker Zoe Louise Parker.

In late February 2001, three young boys were fishing along the Regent's Canal in Camden when they dragged up a heavy bag from the sludge that had been weighed down with bricks. Inside, they found the remains of various body parts belonging to 31-year-old sex worker and mother of two Paula Fields from Liverpool who had been dismembered with a hacksaw.

Body on the bed

With two horrific murders on their hands, police were quick to shut down rumours of a serial killer, but that's exactly what they had on their hands. Paula's boyfriend became the first suspect but there was no evidence against him. Police suggested that the killer had either kept the other parts of her body as a trophy or that there were more body parts in bags throughout the Regent's Canal.

In January 2002, one of Hardy's neighbours called police as she suspected Hardy had vandalised her front door and poured acid through the letter box. When police entered Hardy's flat, they found a locked door but Hardy claimed he didn't have a key to it.

Police broke the door down and found the body of a naked dead woman laying on his bed, covered in cuts and bruises. She was later identified as 38-year-old sex worker Sally White who had been seen with Hardy the night before.

Hardy claimed to have no recollection of how Sally had come to be in his bed, due to his alcohol dependency and mental health issues. While police decided what to do with Hardy, he was transferred to yet another psychiatric hospital where he stayed for 11 months until late November 2002 – just days before the next murder and was allowed to return to his old flat.

Amazingly, the forensic pathologist in the case of Sally White concluded she had died of a heart attack, despite the wounds that Hardy inflicted upon her – which was the sole reason Hardy wasn't charged with Sally's murder. The pathologist would later be struck off the General Medical Council.

Satanic messages

On 30th December, a homeless person was rummaging for food in a Camden bin when he found a black bag containing various body parts. The two women were later identified as 29-year-old Elizabeth Selina Valad and 34-year-old Brigitte MacClennan. Both women were sex workers in and around Camden. Brigitte was ultimately identified through DNA and Elizabeth was identified via the serial number on her breast implants.

A double murder enquiry was launched but police didn't have to look far as Hardy was already on their radar. Investigators found eight more bags containing body parts close to where the first bag had been found. Brigitte's torso was found in a wheelie bin less than 100 metres away.

Hardy's flat was only a few hundred metres from where the body parts had been dumped, which made it easy for police to discover who the suspect was, as they literally followed a trail of blood to Hardy's flat. They obtained a warrant and entered the property but Hardy was nowhere to be seen.

However, the evidence was overwhelming. There was a hacksaw on the kitchen worktop with human skin still attached to it, along with an electric jigsaw power tool, women's shoes and porn magazines everywhere they looked.

A large amount of blood and blood splatter was found in the bathroom with a devil's mask beside the bath, which was worn by Hardy when he killed and cut up his victims. A note on a table in the living room read 'Sally White RIP.'

Satanic messages were written in blood on the walls of the flat along with blood stains on the floor and ceiling. Then police found a number of black bags in the closet containing more body parts, and the torso of Elizabeth. It was suspected that Hardy had sex with the corpses of his victims.

Heads and hands were never found

A large search to hunt Hardy got underway but it was suspected he had fled the area. Three days later on New Year's Day 2003, he was spotted by an off-duty policeman filling in a prescription for his diabetic mediation at University College Hospital.

After a longer than usual wait, Hardy walked outside and attempted to hide behind some bins but two officers approached and got into a fight with him. One was knocked unconscious and the other was stabbed through the hand and had his eye dislocated from his socket. The injured officer was still able to restrain Hardy before back-up arrived and he was finally arrested.

Both Brigitte's and Elizabeth heads and hands were never found and are suspected to either be at the bottom of the Regent's canal or had unknowingly been taken to a waste disposal facility. Another sex worker came forward and said she had been invited back to Hardy's flat around the time of the murders, meaning that Hardy hoped to kill as many as he could.

Following Hardy's arrest, and in the years that followed, there was public outcry as to how Hardy was allowed to kill after being released from mental health care multiple times and not being charged with Sally's murder. Had he been kept in hospital or charged with Sally's murder, then at least two more women would still be alive today.

Hardy pleaded guilty to three counts of murder and was ultimately sentenced to life in prison. He was imprisoned at the specialist Dangerous and Severe Personality Disorder (DSPD) unit at Frankland Prison in County Durham, where he died of sepsis on 26th November 2020, aged 69.

It is strongly believed that Hardy also killed Zoe Louise Parker and Paula Fields. In recent years, he has also been connected to the murders of sex workers Sharon Hoare in 1991 and Christine McGovern in 1995. All four additional murders remain unsolved to this day. If Hardy did kill them, which investigators believe he did, then he could have murdered seven women in total and may be one of Britain's worst serial killers.

Umbrella Murder

While walking across Waterloo Bridge, a Bulgarian writer and journalist was assassinated after being stabbed in the thigh with the poisonous tip of an umbrella, by an assassin codenamed Piccadilly.

In what became known as the Umbrella Murder, 49-year-old Georgi Ivanov Markov was murdered by an unidentified assassin, who used a poisoned pellet hidden in the tip of an umbrella, on Waterloo Bridge, London, in 1978.

Born in 1929, in the Sofia neighbourhood of Knyazhevo in Bulgaria, Markov went on to become a chemical engineer and a technical schoolteacher. After fallen ill with tuberculosis at the age of 19, he was forced to leave his academic career, upon which he turned to writing.

He published his first novel in 1957 and within a few years, was well-known in Bulgaria due to the many awards he was accumulating for his work.

He caught the attention of Bulgarian officials when one of his books was halted mid-publication due to being anti-Lenin, and some of his books were subsequently banned for showing dissent against communism.

Due to his popularity, Markov was one of the authors approached by Bulgarian leader Todor Zhivkov to fill his books with propaganda for the Bulgarian regime. Unlike other authors who were approached, Markov declined, which put him on the Bulgarian watchlist.

Realising he had fallen out with the Bulgarian regime, Markov left the country in 1969 and moved to Italy where his brother lived, intending to return to Bulgaria when the heat on him had died down. In 1971, Bulgarian authorities refused to renew his passport and Markov found himself without a nation. In September of that year, he moved to London, where he would meet his fate.

Listless flock of sheep

Markov picked up the English language quickly and soon found himself working as a journalist for the Bulgarian wing of the BBC World Service. Due to his move to London, in 1972, Markov was suspended from the Union of Bulgarian Writers.

Bulgarian officials had forced the suspension as Markov was seen as a traitor for moving to the West, despite Bulgaria not renewing his passport.

Following on from the suspension, Markov was sentenced to six-and-a-half-years in prison for defection but was tried 'in absentia', meaning he didn't need to be present for the conviction.

After taking time off from the BBC to marry Annabel Dike in 1975 and having one daughter with her, Markov began spreading anti-Bulgarian rhetoric. But he didn't take the campaign against him lying down, in fact, he decided to write and talk about it.

Between 1975 and 1978, Markov penned a series of essays, reports and books about life in communist Bulgaria, including criticisms of the government and their leader Todor Zhivkov. For three years, he continued his criticism of Bulgaria, which in turn, made him an enemy of the state.

'We have seen how personality vanishes, how individuality is destroyed, how the spiritual life of a whole people is corrupted to turn them into a listless flock of sheep.' – Markov.

Despite his very public outrage at the Bulgarian authorities, Markov would confide in friends and colleagues at the BBC that he was in fear of his life and that his words would one day make him a target for assassination. A fear that would soon prove to be true.

Assassination

On 7th September 1978, Markov walked along Waterloo Bridge in London and waited at a bus stop to travel to his job at the BBC. While waiting for the bus, he felt a quick sharp pain on the back of his thigh and turned to see a man holding an umbrella walking away from him.

He watched the man hurriedly cross the road and climb into a taxi but didn't think anymore of the unusual incident until later that day. Initially, Markov had put it down to a clumsy man who hadn't realised what he had done.

A few hours later, while at work at the BBC World Service offices, he realised the pain hadn't gone down and a small red bump had begun to form on the back of his thigh. He took one of his friends and colleagues, Teo Lirkoff, to one side, to tell him what had happened and how unusual it was.

He said that a well-built man with a foreign accent had pushed him in the leg with the point of his umbrella and Markov heard the man say that he was sorry before he walked off. When the workday ended, Markov was in pain and began to feel weak.

Markov barely managed it back to his home in South London where his wife put him to bed. In the middle of the night, he developed a high fever, and due to his deteriorating condition, was admitted to St. James Hospital in Balham.

His symptoms were said to be similar to a bite from a venomous snake but doctors couldn't uncover the cause of the illness. Despite doctors attempting to save his life, Markov died of a massive heart attack four days later on 11th September. It was then that the investigation began.

Death by ricin

The police ordered an autopsy due to the story that Markov had told friends and family. A previous x-ray of Markov's leg had not shown anything untoward. During the autopsy, a tissue sample was taken from the red area on Markov's leg, along with another tissue from the other leg at the same area.

Still, there was nothing unusual showing up, so the samples were sent to the Porton Down chemical and biological weapons laboratory in Wiltshire. One of the medical officers at the facility found a tiny pellet in the tissue sample, which measured less than two millimetres in diameter.

The design of the pellet was seen by some medical officers as flawless. It was composed of 90% platinum and 10% iridium and had two holes drilled through it making an X-like inner hole. The hole would have been filled with poison and covered up with a sugary substance that would have melted once inside Markov's flesh, exposing the poison to his system. The likely poison; ricin.

Ricin is a toxic protein found in the seeds of the castor-oil plant and remains one of the most toxic substances known to man. If one was to chew and ingest castor beans or seeds then they would die within 36 to 72 hours.

The road to death by ricin is not pretty. First come the hallucinations, followed by tightness in the chest, coughing, nausea, severe dehydration, then liver and renal failure. The lungs begin to fail and the body's red cells are destroyed, before succumbing to either respiratory or heart failure.

Astonishingly, there is no antidote for ricin poisoning and any treatment given to a sufferer is to make their last few hours as comfortable as possible. But Markov wasn't the first to be injected with a ricin-filled pellet.

Previous attack

Ten days before Markov's murder, former head of the Paris Bureau of the Bulgarian State Radio and TV network, Vladimir Kostov, was attacked in a similar fashion, as he was leaving the Arc de Triomphe Metro station in Paris.

On August 27th, Kostov heard a crack that sounded like an airgun and felt a sharp pain on the right side of his back. The wound became inflamed but he recovered in hospital and survived. Kostov was also a Bulgarian defector.

In Kostov's case, the pellet had been removed from his back but any poisonous material inside the pellet did not spread as the sugary substance covering the holes didn't melt. The two pellets were later examined in London and it was discovered they were exactly the same size and had the same details, meaning the same assassin was likely to be responsible.

The umbrella murder made headlines all over the world, due to its James Bond style operation, and that the death had come towards the end of the Cold War. The story remained in the headlines for months, forcing a public enquiry into what had happened.

The nature of the assassination meant that Soviet KGB or Bulgarian secret services were suspected of being involved in the attack, which meant that a foreign state had committed murder on British soil, causing controversy across the board.

In early 1979, the enquiry concluded that Markov had died a slow and painful death as a result of a rare poison seeping into his bloodstream. But the enquiry did not conclude with a verdict of murder or manslaughter as it was deemed possible that Markov could have poisoned himself.

Codename Piccadilly

The conclusion of the enquiry again made international headlines as no one else believed that Markov had killed himself in such a fashion, and over time, they were proved right. Many years later, a KGB defector named Oleg Kalugin claimed that the KGB had arranged the murder and had been given options including a jelly to rub on Markov's skin.

Kalugin went onto confirm that Markov had been killed with an umbrella gun. 15 years later, the Times newspaper published an article in which they believed the assassin was an Italian named Francesco Gullino, a known smuggler given the choice of going to a Bulgarian prison or becoming a secret agent in the West, specifically Britain.

In 1993, Gullino was arrested by British and Danish police in Copenhagen and admitted to being in London when Markov was murdered but denied any involvement. Shortly after his release, Gullino eloped and remained off the grid – until August 2021 when he was found dead in an apartment in Austria.

In 2008, due to public interest, British police reopened the Markov file and travelled to Bulgaria, which had ended its communist rule way back in 1990. Investigators managed to speak to various individuals and uncovered secret police files from the time that identified Markov's killer as an agent code-named 'Piccadilly'.

Markov's murder continues to fascinate and intrigue due to the clandestine nature of the story, and there is an exhibit on display at the International Spy Museum in Washington that shows an umbrella gun similar to the one used to kill Markov. To this day, the identity of 'Piccadilly' remains a mystery.

Brighton Babes in the Wood

Two nine-year-old girls were lured to their deaths by a monster who escaped justice for 32 years due to errors in the way forensics handled the original evidence.

The moniker of Babes in the Wood refers to four separate incidents across Britain, Canada, and the United States. The first, known as the Pine Grove Furnace murders was in Pennsylvania, where in 1934, the bodies of three young girls were found under a blanket in the woods. They were killed by their father who shot himself the next day.

The next was in Vancouver, Canada, in 1953, where the remains of two male children were found in a shallow grave in remote woodland. In early 2022, they were identified as Derek and David D'Alton, who had been killed in 1947 by an unknown murderer.

The first Babes in the Wood murders in Britain happened in 1970, when 11-year-old Susan

Muriel Blatchford and 12-year-old Gary John Hanlon were raped and murdered by Ronald Jebson. He left their bodies in open woodland near Sewardstone, Essex.

Jebson was already serving a life sentence for the murder of another girl in 1974 when he confessed to the Blatchford/Hanlon murders and was sentenced to additional life terms. He died in 2015 and if he hadn't confessed, the murders may not have ever been solved.

The Babes in the Wood murders in this story are perhaps the most infamous and were the ones directly named after the children's tale of the same name. In the 16th Century English children's tale, two children are abandoned in a wood, who then die and are covered with leaves by birds.

On 9th October 1986, two nine-year-old girls, Nicola Fellows and Karen Hadaway, were lured to their deaths by then 20-year-old local roofing contractor, Russell Bishop. But the double murder case which haunted the city, remained unsolved for 32 years.

Last time seen alive

Brighton is one of the largest cities on the South Coast of England, approximately 50 miles south of London, and sometimes known as London-by-the-Sea. It's been home to its fair share of infamous crimes and murders but perhaps none more so than the Babes in the Wood double murder.

Nicola and Karen were school friends who played outside a lot and spent most of their free time together. The best friends lived close to each other in the Brighton suburb of Moulsecoomb, just north of the busier parts of the city.

On Thursday 9th October 1986, they both went home after school before getting changed into their play clothes and meeting each other outside. At around 5pm, just an hour before the girls were due to go home for dinner, Nicola's mother, Susan, saw her daughter and Karen playing with their roller skates.

It was the last time that Susan would see her daughter alive. About an hour later at 6pm, a 14-year-old neighbour saw the girls near shops in Lewes Road and told them to go home as it was getting late and their parents would be worried.

The girls ignored the 14-year-old, and Nicola was heard saying to Karen that they should go to the local nature reserve of Wild Park, a location they were not allowed to go to by themselves, due to the size of the park, and the possibility of them getting lost in the woods.

Half hour later, at 6.30pm, the girls were still in Lewes Road, beside a police telephone box, but their killer, Russell Bishop, was seen loitering near them. It was the last time the girls were ever seen alive, except by Bishop, who lured them to their deaths.

Wild Park

When dinnertime in the Fellows and Hadaway households had come and gone, the families began to panic. Susan called Karen's mother, Michelle, to find out what had happened but both families were in the dark as they both thought the girls would be at their friend's homes.

In the early evening, Michelle called the police and the girls disappearances were taken seriously, as it was completely out of character for them. As the night darkened, a 200-strong search party was put together involving police and residents of Moulsecoomb.

Bishop joined the search with his dog but deliberately searched in the wrong areas, trying to hide the fact he knew where the girls were. However, as the search went into the following morning, and then the afternoon, the search team at Wild Park were getting closer and Bishop found himself moving closer to the girls.

In the early afternoon of the 10th, two searchers and residents of Moulsecoomb, Kevin Rowland and Matthew Marchant, came across a makeshift den in the woods. They looked inside and found the bodies of Nicola and Karen, lying side by side. They had been raped and strangled to death.

Despite looking in different locations, when Bishop caught wind that the search team was close to the den, he moved towards it with a purpose. When Rowland and Marchant found the bodies, Bishop ran towards the den with a police officer.

Bishop claimed that he touched the girl's necks to check for a pulse. However, the police officer closest to Bishop at the time the bodies were found, stated that Bishop was too far away to have touched the girls. It was the first of many inconsistencies in Bishop's story that would lead to his arrest.

Bodged prosecution

Bishop told police that he was in Moulsecoomb the evening of the girl's disappearances as he intended to steal a car, which was an odd thing to have admitted to police. He then told other search party members that he had gone to a newsagent to buy a newspaper but realised he had no money and went home.

When interviewed by detectives, he told a different story, and said that he was going to visit his teenage girlfriend but didn't show up as he had got high on cannabis and went home instead. Bishop became one of the prime suspects in the case but the police had worryingly little evidence to go on, despite it being public knowledge that Bishop took a liking to young teenage girls.

His claim of touching the girls necks upon their discovery meant he would have left fingerprint evidence, something that would help in his case, despite the officer claiming he was nowhere near. Still, with all the other inconsistencies, Bishop was arrested on Halloween of the same year and charged with both murders.

His trial, over a year later in December 1987, would prove to be one of the greatest miscarriages of justice Brighton had ever seen, and it was all down to a bodged prosecution, in which a series of errors were made.

Firstly, the pathologist and forensic team failed to take the temperature of the bodies and could not accurately give a time of death, which played havoc with witness statements. The prosecution merely suggested the girls had been killed between 5.15pm and 6.30pm but could not back it up with forensic evidence.

It meant that all of Bishop's alibis could not be argued as he claimed to have been away from Lewes Road and Wild Park by that time. With no witness statements seeing him beyond 6.15pm, they couldn't conclusively prove that Bishop was in Wild Park, and the blunders didn't stop there.

Biggest flaws

Further forensic mistakes helped bolster Bishop's defence that he wasn't the killer. Despite both girls being strangled to death, the hand marks around their necks were never measured and fingerprints were never lifted at the scene, only later at the autopsies, which by that point, there were numerous fingerprints, including Bishop's. Forensic experts also failed to analyse blood that was discovered on Karen's underwear, which may have helped convict the killer. The prosecution then tried to push a blue sweatshirt as a key piece of evidence.

The sweatshirt, they believed Bishop was wearing at the time of the murders, was found discarded near a railway track in Moulsecoomb. Police had a written statement from Bishop's girlfriend, Jennifer Johnson, in that she claimed the sweatshirt belonged to Bishop. With Bishop denying the sweatshirt belonged to him, the prosecution thought they had a damning testimony that proved he was lying.

When Johnson took the stand, she denied having ever seen the sweatshirt before, and gave testimony that she had never mentioned the sweatshirt in the statement, and that it had been fabricated by police and her signature forged, in order for the police to secure a conviction.

But the biggest flaw in the prosecution's case was the time of death, because they simply didn't have one, at least not backed up by scientific evidence. The judge in the trial told the jury that unless they were sure the girls were dead by 6.30pm then they should acquit Bishop. However, there were witness statements that put the girls and Bishop in Lewes Road at 6.30pm which meant the girls were not killed before 6.30pm, meaning the jury's hand was forced. Bishop was acquitted of both the rapes and murders of both girls and went on to sell his story as a wrongfully accused man to The News of the World newspaper for £15,000.

Devil's Dyke attack

The acquittal meant that the double murder case remained open and the investigation looked elsewhere for their suspects. It materialised afterwards that Bishop had gone to Nicola's house the afternoon of their disappearance to talk to his friend, Dougie Judd, who was a lodger who lived there but Nicola had told him to go away.

In The News of the World article, both Bishop and his girlfriend accused a family member from one of the girl's families of being involved. They believed that Barrie Fellows, Nicola's father, was guilty and that they had been set up by police as they were under pressure to find a suspect.

As the Babes in the Wood murders fell under the banner of the coldest of the cold, investigators looked at all possibilities. Bishop's friend, Dougie, and Barrie Fellows were arrested for the murders at various points over the years but there was no evidence linking them, aside from circumstantial.

Four years after the murders, in 1990, a seven-year-old girl was kidnapped and raped at Devil's Dyke in Brighton. She was strangled and left for dead but went on to survive the attack and point out her attacker to police; it was none other than Bishop.

He was found guilty of the attack and sentenced to life in prison with a minimum term of 14 years but at both parole hearings, he was denied release, and 32 years later, would be found guilty of the murders of Nicola and Karen. And it all happened because of a change in the law, specifically relating to the double-jeopardy rule.

Advancements in DNA technology

A new ruling in 2005, changed the double-jeopardy rule which meant a suspect could face a new trial if substantial new evidence came to light. But in 2006, the courts decided there was not enough new evidence to charge Bishop in a second trial for the murders.

In 2012, a new forensics team were given access to the evidence in the case, re-examined it, and discovered DNA evidence. They proved that the sweatshirt did belong to Bishop and found traces of his DNA on material taken from Karen's body.

Bishop was arrested while in prison in 2016 and charged with the murders, 30 years after the fact. A year later, an appeals court removed the acquittals from the 1987 trial which meant that Bishop could be charged at a second trial.

In December 2018, Bishop was found guilty of the murders of Nicola and Karen and sentenced to two additional life sentences with a minimum tariff of 36 years. The trial was only possible because of advancements in DNA technology, and that evidence from the case had been so well stored.

In May 2021, Bishop's ex-girlfriend, Jennifer Johnson, was found guilty of perjury after she admitted lying about Bishop's ownership of the sweatshirt. She was sentenced to six years in prison. On 20th January 2022, Bishop was rushed to hospital where he died of complications with cancer.

The Babes in the Wood case goes to show how entire trials can go either way on the smallest pieces of evidence. Had Jennifer confirmed the sweatshirt belonged to Bishop, and had forensics done their jobs properly, then Bishop would have been convicted sooner, meaning he wouldn't have been free to attack the seven-year-old girl in 1990.

Though there are a number of murders given the moniker of Babes in the Wood, there is none more heinous and infamous than the Brighton murders, of two innocent friends playing with each other in the park, only to have their innocence and lives ripped away by a monster.

The Brink's-Mat Robbery

A gang of armed robbers stole £26milllion of gold bullion, causing a trail of bloodshed and stupidity, in which only two men were convicted of direct involvement, with much of the gold still missing.

Thieves and robbers in Britain are plentiful but only really make the headlines when the amount stolen numbers in the millions. Perhaps the most famous heist, outside of the Great Train Robbery in 1963, is the Brink's-Mat Robbery, 20 years later, in 1983.

The tale of the largest gold bullion heist in British history is littered with bloodshed, stupidity, manhunts, murder, and dishonour amongst thieves, in a cautionary story that even involves a curse placed on those involved.

At 6.40am on 26th November 1983, a gang of six armed robbers in balaclavas broke into the

Brink's-Mat warehouse at Unit 7 on the Heathrow International Trading Estate next to Heathrow Airport in London. Bizarrely, one of them, Mad McAvoy, was wearing a yellow balaclava with a trilby hat and would later wish the tied up security guards a merry Christmas before leaving.

The gang were expecting to find a vault filled with £3million in cash but instead stumbled upon a large amount of gold bullion, almost three tons (3,000kg), that was worth nearly ten times as much.

At the time, the heist was the highest single-value armed robbery in the world, worth £26million in 1983, which equates to around £100million in today's money. And it all happened at a serene warehouse just outside Heathrow Airport, London.

Recruitment

In mid-1983, a group of men came up with a plan to rob the warehouse because of their inside man, Anthony Black. He had informed his brother-in-law, Brian Robinson that there would be £3.2million in cash in the vault overnight on November 25th, and that he would help him get them in by opening the door in return for a share of the money.

Robinson had a history of armed robbery and was known as The Colonel to those that knew him. His childhood friend, Tony White, who had just been released from prison after spending 12 years inside for another heist in 1970, was recruited to help with the Brink's-Mat job.

Brian then recruited his friend and known South London gangster Micky 'Mad' McAvoy, who was prone to outbursts of anger and violence. It was later suggested that McAvoy became the ringleader of the robbery and got to organising the entire heist from his council house.

McAvoy brought in George Francis, an associate who was known for armed robbery and drugs smuggling, having once smuggled a large amount of cannabis from Pakistan hidden among containers of clothing packages.

After Francis was recruited, McAvoy's closest friend, Brian Perry, was brought in on the deal to assist in the robbery. Though never confirmed, White, Francis and Perry were only ever suspected of being involved in the gang. The other person directly involved in the robbery has never been identified.

A job robbers dreamed about

At 6.30am on that morning, five security guards turned up for their shifts at the estate and were tasked with transporting the gold to the airport as part of a scheduled delivery to Hong Kong and the Philippines. Black turned up a few minutes late for work but had already given the gang a key to the building.

He let them in through the main security door then informed the other guards that he was going to use the loo. The armed robbers then slipped into the main building and overpowered the guards, hitting some in the head with their guns and handcuffing them.

McAvoy doused some of the guards in petrol and threatened to set them alight if they tried to stop them or if the robbery didn't go as planned. Due to Black's insider information, the gang were able to navigate the building with ease and knew where many of the external and internal security cameras were.

They forced the guards to give them the combination numbers to the vault and opened it expecting to find £3.2million in cash. The cash was there in plain sight but alongside it were almost 7,000 gold bars, each about the size of a Mars bar.

The gang stopped in their tracks and had to work things out quick. The original plan was to be in and out of the warehouse within ten minutes, but those ten minutes turned into almost two hours when they decided to take all the gold with them.

The problem was that they hadn't planned for the weight of the gold and arrived in a Ford transit van that was only going to be comfortable for six people and bags of money, not boxes of heavy gold, which was estimated to weigh in the region of 3,000 kilograms (three tons).

They used the warehouse's forklift truck to load the gold into the van, separated into cases used for transporting bullion on aircraft. It was one of those jobs that robbers dreamed about; expecting a certain amount of loot only to be met with, quite literally, a goldmine.

Somehow, they managed to fill the van with all the gold and one of the robbers turned to the guards as he was leaving and said, *'thanks ever so much for your help. Have a very nice Christmas, boys.'*

Immediate problems

Despite the longer time it had taken – it was shortly before 8.15am when they left the warehouse – they managed to get away with it, until the van stalled a couple of roads away. Realising the warehouse was only around the corner, the gang panicked until they finally got it started.

The van was so overloaded that the metal frame would occasionally scrape along the tarmac road until they found more suitable transport. The van would become the first of many problems because the gang wanted cash, not gold, and they had no idea what to do with it.

Along with the 3,000kg of gold bullion and just over £3million in cash, they also had over £100,000 worth of cut and uncut diamonds. The gold was owned by Johnson Matthey Bankers

Ltd., who were in the process of sending the gold to the East. The company, founded in 1817, collapsed the following year after handing out loans to fraudsters and firms who went bankrupt immediately, but they reorganised the company and are now part of the FTSE 250, as one of the biggest companies in Britain.

At around 8.30am, one of the guards broke free of his restraints and raised the alarm, and as newspapers broke the story around the world, the gang were put under pressure to shift not only the cash but the gold. Little did they know but the amount they had stolen immediately put them on Britain's rich list and they owned more than some third-world countries at the time.

In the days that followed, the gang approached an underworld figure known only as The Fox, due to having no idea how to sell off the gold. By that point, Scotland Yard's Flying Squad, known informally as The Sweeney, were hunting the band of merry bandits.

Realising the gang must have had insider information, the investigation turned to the security guards, and Black was pointed out as a suspect due to him arriving late and using the loo straight away. When Black was brought in for questioning two days later, he denied having anything to do with the robbery but mentioned that police should be looking at his brother-in-law, Robinson – virtually giving him up straight away.

Goldfinger

When the investigation looked at Robinson, they made the connection to McAvoy and put them both under surveillance. McAvoy wasn't the most modest or careful of criminals and within a week of the robbery had moved from his humble council house to a countryside mansion that he paid for with cash.

Robinson had done the same, moving out of his South London home to a country estate which was again paid for in cash. McAvoy also purchased two Rottweiler dogs and called them Brink and Mat, which was probably not the wisest thing to have done when he was meant to be laying low.

With assistance from The Fox, the gang were put in contact with various money launderers and jewellers, in an attempt to melt down the gold. Just two days after the robbery, an elderly couple in Bath, Somerset, noticed their neighbour using a large ceramic crucible, an item traditionally used to melt materials at high temperature.

Police arrived at the couple's home and informed them that their neighbour's home fell under the jurisdiction of another police force and they couldn't investigate. They claimed to have passed the report on to the other force, but police didn't turn up at the home for another 14 months.

The home in question belonged to local gold dealer, John Palmer, who was given the moniker of 'Goldfinger' by the British press, when it turned out he was involved in melting down some of the Brink's-Mat gold. When a warrant was issued for his arrest 14 months later, he eloped to Tenerife with his family.

Palmer was extradited to the UK a few years later but had his trial acquitted as he confessed to melting down gold at the time but had no idea it was from the Brink's-Mat robbery. His name would be one of dozens who were indirectly involved in the robbery.

The game's up

11 days after the robbery, police had enough evidence against Robinson and McAvoy that they raided their home and arrested them, along with White who was linked to Robinson and who had just come out of prison for a previous armed robbery.

Robinson and McAvoy were picked out of a line-up by the security guards but White wasn't and he was acquitted at his trial. In December 1984, Robinson and McAvoy were sentenced to 25 years in prison for their parts in masterminding the robbery. To this day, they have never given up the names of who were with them on the job itself.

It's only in recent years that White, Francis, and Perry were suspected of being the other three. Perry and Francis were known to have been in control of the bullion soon after and recruited VAT fraudster and launderer Kenneth Noye to help them shift the gold.

Between them they recruited more people including criminal financier Gordon Parry and bent solicitor Michael Relton. They set up off-shore accounts, recycled the money and invested in property and businesses.

When McAvoy's mistress, Kathy Meacock, went to visit him in prison, she boasted about a new country house in a magazine that she owned. A nosy prison officer overheard the conversation and reported it. Police discovered that the house had been purchased through an off-shore account via Relton.

They also learned that McAvoy's wife also purchased property through Relton and was known to be having an affair with Perry behind McAvoy's back. When Perry was arrested and interviewed by police, he admitted to handling the gold and said he had lost control of it and couldn't get it back as he had no idea where it was.

The Noye connection

Perry was sentenced to nine years in 1992 for handling the stolen gold as it couldn't be proven he was one of the six robbers. Relton got 12 years for money laundering and fraud, and Parry got ten years for handling stolen goods.

Investigators quickly learned that £26million of gold was somewhere in the UK but they had no idea where and due to the amount of people that were being recruited to help shift it, the original gang members had lost sight of the gold.

Noye had helped melt down half of the gold and recast some of it for resale, mixing in copper coins to disguise the source of the metals. In late 1984, Noye and another criminal, Brian Reader, shifted around £10million of funds through a Bristol bank which set alarms off at the Bank of England, who informed the police.

In 1985, an undercover police officer was keeping tabs on Noye and hiding in his garden, when Noye spotted him and stabbed him to death. At the trial for the officer's murder, Noye was found not guilty as the officer didn't identify himself and could have been seen as an intruder.

However, in 1986, Noye was found guilty of handling stolen goods and sentenced to 14 years. Around the same time, Reader was sentenced to nine years for his part in handling the stolen gold. Noye served seven years and was released in 1994.

Noye caught the attention of the British public again in 1996, when he murdered Stephen Cameron during a road rage incident. He fled to the Costa Del Sol in Spain but was extradited back the UK in 2000 where he was sentenced to life in prison for the murder. But the bloodshed and fallout from the robbery didn't end there.

The bodies fall

The fallout from the robbery and resulting incidents led the job to be referred to as the Brink's-Mat curse. Reader, who was sentenced to nine years for handling stolen goods, would later become the mastermind for the £14million Hatton Garden heist in 2015. He was released from prison in 2018 after just three years due to bad health and having only served half his sentence.

Goldfinger Palmer left Britain entirely after his acquittal and built a £300million fortune via a timeshare scam in Tenerife and Spain. He was shot dead at one of his home's in Essex in June 2015 by an unidentified assassin.

After serving his sentence, Perry went on to build a London minicab empire but was shot dead in South London in 2001. Two years later, Francis, who was one of the suspected six robbers, was shot dead by assassins in Bermondsey. Their murders have never been solved. Other people directly or indirectly linked to the robbery were also targeted.

In 1987, ex-cop Dan Morgan was found murdered, and supposedly had tenuous links to the gang. In the same year, a detective on the case, Alan Holmes, allegedly took his own life. In 1990, Nick Whiting, who was suspected of being a snitch for the police was shot dead. Four years after that, gun dealer Sidney Wink allegedly took his own life, and was suspected of having supplied the guns for the robbery. In 1995, a known associate of Noye, Pat Tate, was shot dead with two other men in Essex. A few months later, a drug dealer known to have used funds from the gold to make deals was also found dead. And we can keep going...

Robbery to drugs

In the same year, Donald Urquhart, a known money launderer was shot dead by an assassin in West London. In 1996, another associate of Noye, John Marshall, was shot dead in Sydenham, South London. In the same year, money launderer Keith Hedley was killed by three men while he was relaxing on his yacht in Corfu.

A bullion smelter and financier name Solly Nahome, supposedly linked to the heist, was shot dead outside his North London home in 1998. A month later, a gangland enforcer, Gilbert Wynter, disappeared and was suspected to have been murdered, with his remains buried in the foundations of the O2 Arena in London, then known as the Millennium Dome.

In 2000, a witness named Alan Decabral, who was about to testify against Noye was assassinated as he sat in his parked car in Ashford, Kent. In Spain, in 2007, crime boss Joey Wilkins was shot dead during a robbery of his home. He was known to have named Noye in regard to the robbery.

Many other deaths have been indirectly linked to the robbery. During the ecstasy rage of the 1990s and early 2000s, many people died from taking ecstasy, and the drugs had entered the country with the use of funds filtered down from the Brink's-Mat robbery.

Tentacles

Robinson served his time in prison and went straight, setting up a cheque to cash business and opening a wine bar. It remained unclear where he was getting his funds from. He died of natural causes in March 2021, without a penny to his name. McAvoy served his sentence and moved to Spain.

Relton and Parry are believed to be in hiding somewhere in the United States and other people indirectly involved in the robbery are living in fear. It has never been made known who The Fox was nor what happened to the bulk of the gold but someone, somewhere, got very rich off it.

It is suggested that the Brink's-Mat robbery had such an impact on the British gold industry that anyone wearing gold jewellery in the UK after 1983, is likely wearing Brink's-Mat gold, which is an extraordinary revelation.

An unidentified gang member contacted the press many years later and said that none of the gold remained in Britain, instead being shipped off to the Philippines as the order to rob the gold had come from high-ranking officials in the country. Other researchers and investigators believe that around £10million of the gold is buried in farmyards and scrap metal yards but with so many deaths linked to it, it's perhaps not worth digging out the metal detector to hunt down.

The truth is, that the tentacles of the robbery spread to virtually every corner of the globe and the repercussions and links to so many people is still being felt. It's clear that much of the gold was melted down and laundered to create vast wealth but where it happened and who really became wealthy from it, remains unknown to this day.

The Hungerford Massacre

In one of the deadliest mass shootings in Britain, a lone wolf went on a day-long spree, killing 16 people and leaving a quaint English market town looking like a war zone, in a case that changed gun laws.

On 19th August 1987, a fanatical gun fan, Michael Ryan, went on a rampage in the small market town of Hungerford, Berkshire. Carrying an automatic rifle, a pistol, and at least one hand grenade, he killed 16 people and injured 15 in Britain's worst mass shooting.

The fallout of the massacre changed the country's gun laws forever, banning the ownership of automatic and semi-automatic weapons and restricting the use of shotguns with a capacity of more than three cartridges.

To add to the tragedy, Ryan killed himself after the attacks, denying the families of the dead and the British public a motive for the killings. Born in May 1960, Ryan was the only child of building inspector Alfred Ryan, and his wife, school dinner lady and waitress Dorothy Ryan.

Ryan's father died two years before the massacre in 1985, aged 80, leading some to suspect his death might have been the catalyst for the spree. In the Spring of 1987, Ryan took employment as a labourer working on fences and footpaths near the River Thames.

He left the job three months later in July and became unemployed, seeking help from the state in the form of unemployment benefits. Only one month later, Ryan would walk through Hungerford dressed in army camo gear, firing at anyone he saw.

Savernake

On that fateful day, 35-year-old Susan Godfrey decided it was a good day to go for a picnic and travelled with her two young children from Reading to Savernake Forest in Wiltshire, seven miles from Hungerford.

They were preparing their picnic amongst the trees when Susan saw Ryan walking towards them carrying guns. Immediately panicked, Susan put the children in her car and locked the doors but Ryan had caught up to them quickly and abducted Susan at gunpoint.

He led her into the forest where he had laid down a tarpaulin groundsheet, leading police to believe he had intended to rape her. Instead, Ryan shot her in the chest, and as she crawled away from the groundsheet, he put another 12 bullets into her, killing her instantly.

A hiker in the woods found the screaming children in the car a few minutes later, and called police but by that point, Ryan was already on his way to Hungerford. Halfway between Savernake Forest and Hungerford, he pulled into a petrol station and calmly filled his car and a petrol can.

He waited for the only other customer to leave before opening fire at the cashier, Kakoub Dean, from the forecourt. He then entered the shop and pointed his gun at Kakoub's head. When he pulled the trigger, the gun jammed, he grimaced and walked out the store to drive away, leaving Kakoub shaking in fear.

She called the police who sent three patrol cars to the station, but by that point, Ryan was already in Hungerford, on his way to infamy.

Opening fire

Around 15 minutes later, off-duty police officer, Trevor Wainwright, was on his way to his part-time gardening job when he heard of an attempted armed robbery at the petrol station. Trevor was one of a handful of officers based in Hungerford.

The police team included two sergeants and 12 constables on the station list, but on duty on 19th August were one sergeant, two constables and one station duty officer – not enough to handle the massive influx of calls and incidents that were about to come in.

Deciding that the petrol station was a few miles outside of his jurisdiction, and believing it would be handled by other officers, he continued his gardening job at the home of Mrs. Roland-Clarke. Half hour later, Roland-Clarke said there was a call for him. His wife was on the phone in a panicked state, claiming that someone was firing a weapon close to where they lived.

Ryan had arrived at his home at approximately 12.45pm when neighbours heard gunshots, and later learned that he had shot dead the two family dogs. He was spotted leaving the house with ammunition and dressed in survival and camo gear, including a bullet-proof vest.

After failing to start his car, he returned to his home with the petrol can and set light to the living room and kitchen before heading east towards the local common. On his way to the common, he killed two of his neighbours, Roland and Sheila Mason. He shot Roland six times in the chest and Sheila once in the head.

A 14-year-old girl, Lisa Mildenhall, ran from her nearby home to see what was going on and Ryan turned to face her. He pointed the automatic rifle at her head before lowering it and shooting her four times in the legs. Fortunately, Lisa would go on to recover from her injuries as first aid was administered by her parents and neighbours.

An elderly lady named Dorothy Smith, who was standing outside of her home, saw Ryan walk past and called out to him, saying, *'stop what you're doing, you're scaring everybody to death.'* Ryan smirked and carried on walking without shooting her.

He then shot another neighbour, Marjorie Jackson, in the back, but she survived the shooting. By this point, Trevor had rushed back to his home, which was on a nearby street, and saw smoke billowing from the houses.

War zone

Then he noticed people cowering in their doorways, some laying deathly still, and others crying for help. At first, he thought the armed robbers from the petrol station were on the run and killing people at random but when he asked one of the residents what was going on, the reply was; *'some bloke's gone mad with a gun.'*

Trevor ordered his wife and anyone who could hear him to stay indoors and then he ran to Hungerford town centre where he collected some maps of the town before heading to the police station. The maps were going to be used for the armed response team that he hoped were already on their way.

Linda Chapman was driving her daughter Alison to her friend's house on the street where the shootings had started. When she turned the corner into the street, her car was shot at by Ryan but she managed to drive away without any major injuries.

Responding to the crisis, an ambulance was on its way to help residents, with paramedics Linda Bright and Hazel Haslett. As soon as they turned the corner, Ryan opened fire, injuring Haslett. Bright managed to immediately put the vehicle into reverse and retreated into the driveway of a nearby home.

The fire engine called out to stop the blaze at Ryan's home was blocked by police and other cars, but by that point, the fire had spread to two neighbouring properties, and suddenly, it felt like Hungerford was at war.

At the police station, panic had set in with local residents having stormed the station to call for help and the station were being redirected 999 calls that they couldn't deal with. The minimal officers on duty could not go into the so-called danger zone because it was already too dangerous for them.

Killing his mother

Trevor put himself on duty but he was already in a losing situation. Police cars were already near the danger zone, busy getting people to safety and preventing any pedestrians or cars moving into the location where Ryan was thought to be heading.

Two of Trevor's colleagues were following up on a lead that Ryan had continued west towards the school, when they were shot at by Ryan who was walking beside a residential garden. One of the officers, who had just got out of the car, ran to safety inside a nearby home.

The other officer, Jeremy Wood, escaped in his car with a resident and parked up at the common where he begged the station to get hold of the Thame's Valley Police Tactical Firearms Unit. But that officer, and Trevor, learned that help wasn't coming anytime soon, as the armed unit were still 60km away on a training exercise. It would be an entire hour before they arrived in Hungerford.

Marjorie Jackson, who had been shot in the back, managed to phone her husband, Ivor, who was rushing back to Hungerford from his work, driven by colleague George White. As they got close to the street, Ryan opened fire on their car with eleven bullets, hitting Ivor in the chest and head and George in the head, killing George as their car crashed at high speed into an abandoned police car.

Ryan's mother, Dorothy, was on her way back to the town from a shopping trip when she saw the incident with Ivor and George. She got out of her car and checked on Ivor who was still breathing and would later go on to survive the attack.

Dorothy ran up the street to find houses on fire, people lying dead in gardens and on the roadside, and car crashes lining the street. In the middle of the chaos, she saw her son holding a gun in his hand. Ivor heard Dorothy say, '*stop, Michael. Why are you doing this?*'

Ryan traipsed towards his mother, raised his beretta pistol, and shot her twice at point blank range, and another two times as she fell to the ground, killing her instantly. Then he moved to Hungerford Common and the War Memorial Grounds, where he continued his rampage.

Rampage

Many residents had heard the commotion but couldn't hear what was going on and went about their daily business on the common and outside of the danger zone. A police helicopter had located Ryan and were ordering him to stop firing using the speaker system but he ignored them.

While walking through the common, he shot dead a 26-year-old dog walker, a taxi driver who was on his way to the hospital to visit his newborn son, and shot at a teenager on a bicycle, along with a man who was sitting in his parked van listening to the news.

Some residents exited their homes to see what was going on and were shot by Ryan in the process. A car driving towards Ryan was shot at, killing Douglas Wainwright and injuring his wife, Kathleen. At the police station, news that the armed unit were close brought a glimmer of hope to the situation but Trevor was called into his superior's office.

Expecting to be lambasted for not wearing his police uniform, he was met with unfortunate news. Douglas, his father, had been killed. Trevor raced to the hospital to see his mother and was informed that Douglas was actually still alive but would later die of his injuries.

At around the same time, two more cars were shot at and any resident Ryan laid eyes on were also shot at with many more killed. With the armed unit setting up a command centre in Hungerford, all resources turned to stopping the madman.

The police helicopter, along with following Ryan, were broadcasting warnings to the public to stay inside and lock their doors. Ryan ignored all the warnings from the helicopter and arrived at John O'Gaunt School, which was closed for the Summer holidays, and where he had once been a pupil.

Britain's bloodiest day

Sensing the opportunity to trap him, the armed units and local officers began securing homes and gardens close to the school before surrounding it entirely by 4pm. An hour later, a sergeant with the armed unit, Paul Brightwell, spoke to Ryan, who claimed he still had weapons and a grenade.

Ryan wanted to know if his mother was dead or alive as he felt as though killing her was a mistake. He also told Brightwell that '*Hungerford must be in a bit of a mess.*' Brightwell spoke to Ryan for the best part of 90 minutes but was unable to ascertain a motive for the spree.

At 6.45pm, Ryan said, '*I wish I had stayed in bed,*' before adding, '*it's funny, I killed all those people but I haven't got the guts to blow my own brains out.*' But just seven minutes later, he did, shooting himself in the head and ending Britain's bloodiest day. Ryan had killed 16 people and seriously injured 15.

While Trevor was in the hospital with his mother, he heard on the news that the killer was Michael Ryan, but for the life of him, he couldn't place the name. A few minutes later, it clicked, and he realised all too well who Ryan was. Trevor was the officer who had carried out the checks for Ryan's firearms licenses.

Ryan had been issued first with a shotgun license in 1978 and eight years later in 1986, was granted a firearms certificate covering the ownership of two pistols. This was later extended to three, and one month before the spree, a license was issued to cover two semi-automatic weapons. By the time of the massacre, he had licenses allowing him to possess eight guns.

Motive went with him to the grave

Following on from the massacre and a public outpouring of grief, the Hungerford Report was commissioned by the British Government which introduced the Firearms (Amendment) Act 1988. The new law banned ownership of semi-automatic weapons and restricted the use of shotguns with a capacity of more than three cartridges.

Without Ryan directly telling anyone the motive for his spree, researchers were led to conclude he was suffering from undiagnosed mental health issues. This, combined with a hatred against the world after his father's death, led him to going on a spree, though it is generally agreed he hadn't intended to go on a spree but once he got started, he simply carried on.

For Trevor, he believed that by approving the checks on Ryan's licenses, he had signed his own father's death warrant, despite following the letter of the law. To this day, he remains haunted by the massacre.

Ryan may have been influenced by a mass shooting in Australia that took place 10 days earlier in Melbourne, where a former soldier killed seven people and injured 19, known as the Hoddle Street Massacre.

In the wake of two more British massacres, the Dunblane Massacre in 1996 and the Cumbria Shootings in 2010, access by the general public to firearms in the United Kingdom is subject to some of the strictest control measures in the world.

Aside from special permission granted to farmers and hunters, guns are completely banned. The Hungerford Massacre is known as the deadliest mass shooting in peacetime Britain and was caused by a lone wolf whose motive went with him to the grave.

Saturday Night Strangler

A Welsh serial killer who raped and killed three girls in Port Talbot in 1973 on Saturday nights, was caught 30 years later – after his death – in the first case in history solved using familial DNA testing.

There are very few Welsh serial killers but one who always tops the list is Joseph William Kappen, AKA: The Saturday Night Strangler, so called as he claimed his victims on Saturday nights across Port Talbot in 1973.

He was additionally linked to the unsolved murder of 23-year-old Maureen Mulcahy in Aberavon in 1976, who had left friends to meet an unidentified acquaintance. Her strangled body was found in woodland the next day. Her murder remains unsolved and is still a cold case in Wales.

Kappen is so notorious in Wales that he was the country's first most documented serial killer but as fate would have it, he wouldn't be caught until after his death, when familial DNA testing linked him to the murders, the first time in history it had been used to identify a serial killer and solve a case.

Kappen was born in 1941 and remained in Port Talbot for most of his life. He was raised by his stepfather after his parents split up and was one of seven siblings. Due to the fallout from his parent's divorce, he turned to petty crime, and by the age of 13 was already known to local police for a number of minor thefts.

Into his late teens and early twenties, he garnered over thirty convictions for theft, burglary, and assault, and would spend most of his formative years in and out of prison. He could never hold down a job for longer than a few months and was known as a loner.

When he was 21, he met 17-year-old Christine Powell and they married two years later. Ten days after the marriage, Kappen was sent to prison for burglary. When he was released a few months later, Kappen became abusive and would abuse and rape Christine on many occasions, a sign of things to come.

Hunting young girls

They had a daughter and son together but it didn't stop Kappen from continuing to abuse his younger wife. At one point, while walking the family dog, he strangled it to death in front of his son, claiming that death was the only way, as the dog was old.

Despite his marriage, Kappen found himself attracted to young teenage girls, who he could project his controlling influence onto. He got a job as a bouncer at local bars and clubs which put him in direct contact with them.

In 1964, after being released from a burglary sentence, he sexually assaulted a 15-year-old girl but she was able to fight him off and escape, but Kappen wasn't identified as the attacker and he was free to search for his first murder victim.

In early 1973, a few months before the murders, Kappen picked up two female hitchhikers then drove them to an isolated lane where he attempted to rape them. They too managed to escape but didn't report it, which led to Kappen moving from attempted rape to murder in order to get what he wanted.

On Saturday 14th July 1973, 16-year-old Sandra Newton and her friends went out drinking in Briton Ferry, a small town in Port Talbot. They visited the local nightclub but got split up, and by the end of the night, Sandra found herself needing a lift back home.

Realising it was a perfect time to hunt for young girls, Kappen found Sandra hitchhiking on the side of the road and lured her into his car. He drove her to the grounds of a rural coal mine a few miles away, dragged her out of the car and raped her before strangling her to death with her own skirt.

Top Rank

Kappen didn't attempt to hide the body and dumped Sandra near a water tunnel close to the coal mine. Her body was found three days later, sparking a murder investigation that simply went nowhere. Police suspected the man was local due to having knowledge of the water tunnel but could not pin down a suspect.

Two months later, 16-year-old friends Geraldine Hughes and Pauline Floyd went out clubbing in Swansea, ten miles away from Port Talbot. At that time in history, the term serial killer was still to become public knowledge, and the girls assumed that the murder of Sandra was a one-off that wouldn't happen to anyone else. They were wrong.

After visiting a number of local bars, they went to the Top Rank nightclub in the city and danced through the night until the early hours, when instead of getting a taxi back home, they decided to hitchhike to save money.

Kappen, who was stalking the streets for his victims, noticed the two girls needing a lift and gladly obliged. He drove them to

Llandarcy woods, in-between Swansea and Port Talbot, where he raped both girls and strangled them to death.

Their bodies were found the next morning, and when word got around about the double murder, the community recoiled in fear, as three girls had been killed in the same manner within three months, leading police to believe they had a multiple murderer on their hands.

The investigation learned that both girls were seen getting into a white Austin 1100 which became the focus early on in the case. 150 detectives were brought in to work on the case, and they quickly learned there were an estimated 10,000 male drivers of an Austin 1100 within fifty miles of Port Talbot.

In the days before mobile phones and internet, the command room became swamped in paperwork, making the investigation even more difficult, as some of the detectives ended up redoing work that had already been carried out.

An impossible task

After the Austin 1100, the investigation turned to the giant Port Talbot steelworks, where at least 13,000 men were employed. Every single one of them became a suspect, as most local men worked at the factories.

But at the same time, the nearby M4 motorway was under construction, and many of the crew working on it came from outside the area. There was also the possibility that the killer could have come to town to visit the large annual Neath Fair, which took place the weekend of the murders.

Suddenly, the suspect list grew and grew, and with minimal databasing techniques in place, the investigation began to collapse in on itself, which wasn't helped by the miner's strikes that had forced the government to implement a three-day working week.

During the enquiries relating to the Austin 1100, Kappen's name came up as an owner, and police went to his home to interview him. However, Kappen had removed the wheels of the car to make it look as though it was not roadworthy.

Kappen was reported driving the car at the time of the murders but due to the investigation overload, the report wasn't cross-referenced, and in addition to his wife giving him a false alibi out of fear of his abuse, Kappen was struck off the suspect's list.

By the summer of 1974, the investigation came to an end and the hundreds of boxes of paperwork, admin, and evidence, went into storage at Sandfields police station in Port Talbot. 16 years later in 1990, Dr. Colin Dark of the Chepstow's Forensic Science Services was put on the case, but when he went to visit the storage room, the files had been mostly destroyed by damp and a mice infestation.

Clark was able to anticipate the rise of DNA technology and requested that the physical evidence, including the girl's underwear, should be removed and stored at the Chepstow laboratories for future investigation. It was something that would ultimately solve the case.

Operation Magnum

In 1998, 25 years after the double murder, technology advanced to such a degree that a male fingerprint was found on the underwear which contained genetic material. Two years later in 2000, Clark and his team began searching the national DNA database. The DNA database was set up in 1995 for people arrested on suspicion of a crime or charged with a crime.

If the killer had been arrested or charged since 1995, then his DNA would show up on the system – but it didn't. Due to having the killer's DNA, the original investigation was fully reopened as a cold case that went under the banner of Operation Magnum.

Three ageing detectives took on the case and were tasked with going back through the mouldy evidence, and at the same time, forensic evidence proved that the killer of the two girls also killed Sandra, and they were linked as three murders for the first time.

The operation got their suspect list down to 500 people, out of 35,000 initial suspects, with help from psychological profiles. Due to the difficulty in tracking down the 500 men, due to the age of the facts the team had on record, only 353 were ever tested but none of them matched the DNA.

Kappen was on the list but had died of lung cancer in June 1990. In 2002, the team used a new DNA tactic called familial genetic testing, which assumes family members will have partial matches of the same DNA. They ran it through the new system and found a car thief named Paul Kappen, who was only seven at the time of the murders.

Realising Joseph Kappen was Paul's father, he became the prime suspect. After Kappen's ex-wife and his daughter gave the investigation DNA swabs, the investigation concluded they had found their killer. The Saturday Night Strangler had been caught – after his death.

In the summer of 2002, almost 30 years after the murders, Kappen's body was exhumed and tested, providing a 100% match for the DNA of the killer. In the case of Maureen Mulcahy, who was killed in 1976, there was no DNA material available which could prove either way if Kappen had killed her, but he has long remained the prime suspect, meaning he might have killed at least four young girls.

The Kappen investigation was the first in the world to use familial DNA tracing to identify a killer and solve a previously unsolved murder. The way the case was solved, led to many other cold cases being cracked, and the technology was implemented across the world.

The Monster Butler & The Sidekick

Scottish serial killer Archibald Hall, known as The Monster Butler, killed five people in the late 1970s while working for the British upper class, with help from his sidekick, Kitto.

Archibald Thomson Hall was known as The Monster Butler, who committed his crimes whilst working for the British upper class and killed five people to protect his identity in order to continue his life of luxury.

Born in Glasgow, Scotland, in 1924, Hall began his criminal career at an early age and moved from thieving from local shops to breaking and entering homes in the middle of the night. In his formative years he realised he was bisexual and moved to London where he became well known in the underground gay scene of the 1950s to 1970s.

He was convicted of a jewellery theft in the 1960s and sent to prison for ten years before escaping five years later. He was recaptured and served out his sentence. While there, he studied antiques and learned the etiquette of the aristocracy and upper classes so that he could hide his identity once he was released.

He also took elocution lessons to soften his Scottish accent. He was in and out of prison for various crimes including robbery. In 1975, following on from his most recent release, he moved back to Scotland and used the name Roy Fontaine, named after his favourite actress Joan Fontaine.

Hall was employed as a butler to Margaret Hudson who was the widow of conservative politician Austin Hudson. Margaret lived at the lavish Kirtleton House in Dumfriesshire and Hall was more than happy to work there. He had initially planned to steal the most valuable items in the house and elope.

However, he changed his mind when he realised he really enjoyed working for Margaret and fell in love with being a butler. Then, in 1977, one of Hall's former cellmates, David Wright, was employed as a groundskeeper, which panicked Hall, as Wright knew his true identity.

Killing to hide his identity

While robbing some jewellery, Wright threatened to tell the lady of the house about Hall's previous convictions but Hall liked his job too much for Wright to ruin it all. Hall devised a plan to take Wright on a rabbit hunt under the pretence of coming to an agreement.

While in the woods, Hall shot Wright dead and buried him in a shallow grave next to a stream in the grounds of the estate. But Wright had already told Margaret Hudson of Hall's criminal past, and Hall was fired.

Immediately moving down to Chelsea, London, Hall found work as a butler at the penthouse apartment of retired labour politician Walter Scott-Elliott and his Indian-born wife, Dorothy, who had wealth beyond compare.

Three months into the job, he came up with a plan to rob the Scott-Elliott's of their fortune and elope to a foreign non-extradition country. On 8th December 1977, Hall and an accomplice named Michael Kitto went to the apartment to view the antiques, in order to price things up.

Hall believed that Walter would be in bed and Dorothy was getting treatment at a nearby nursing home but as they discussed their plans of how to cash in the goods and rob the apartment of everything, Dorothy walked in on them – and heard what they were planning.

Kitto and Hall pounced on Dorothy, and Kitto suffocated her to death with a pillow but it has long remained unclear whether Hall was the culprit in her murder. The pair carried her body to the bedroom and put her in bed as if she had died in her sleep.

They then drugged Walter, who was curious to know what had happened to his wife, and he passed out on his bed. The next morning, Kitto and Hall recruited a 51-year-old sex worker named Mary Coggle and came up with an audacious plan.

Bloody road trip

Hall believed they could pass off Coggle as the late Dorothy, hoping that Walter, who would be drugged up, would believe Coggle to be his wife. They put Dorothy's body in the boot of the car the next day and sat Walter next to Coggle in the back seat, then drove north towards Scotland with all of the couple's antiques and riches.

They stopped at various financial establishments where Walter, under guidance from Coggle, emptied the Scott-Elliot bank accounts. They drugged Walter so heavily that he had to be helped to their pit-stop accommodation in Cumbria before travelling to Perthshire the next day. The pair buried Dorothy in a shallow grave and continued northward.

After having Walter sign some documents giving them further access to the Scott-Elliot financial accounts, they drove to Glen Affric in the

Highlands, where Hall and Kitto murdered Walter by strangling and beating him to death. They buried his body in remote woodland near Inverness.

The trio decided to return to London after selling off some of the antiques across Scotland but Coggle was becoming too accustomed to her newfound life of luxury. She took to wearing Dorothy's fur coat everywhere which Hall thought was going to attract attention.

When Coggle refused to get rid of the coat, Hall killed her with a poker stick and left her body in a stream in Dumfriesshire, which was found a few days later on Christmas Day 1977. Hall and Kitto travelled to Hall's holiday home in Cumbria, only to find that Hall's brother, convicted paedophile, Donald, had been released from jail and was sitting in the living room.

Hotel mishap

Hall hated Donald for what he had done to be convicted, so he tied him to a chair, used chloroform to knock him out, then drowned him in the bath with Kitto's help. The murder was later recognised as the first murder resulting from chloroform in the United Kingdom.

The pair put Donald's body in the boot of the car and again drove northward to Scotland, where they checked into the Blenheim House Hotel in

North Berwick, near Edinburgh. As the pair were drinking in the hotel bar, the manager became suspicious of them as they were acting unusually jumpy.

Believing they would elope the following morning without paying, the manager called the police who checked the numberplate of Hall's car. To hide the identity of the owner, Hall had changed the number plate as it contained three nine's which he believed was unlucky.

The police check showed the numberplate, car, and tax disc didn't match, and arrested Kitto, who was taken in for questioning. Hall had managed to escape through a toilet window but was caught shortly after at a police roadblock. Not realising what was in the boot of the car, police moved the vehicle to the storage area of the local police station, where they discovered Donald's body.

At the same time, in London, police were investigating the disappearances of the Scott-Elliot's and a suspected robbery that had taken place in their apartment. Police in Scotland traced the car to London and linked up with London police, connecting both crimes.

The not-so perfect gentleman

Soon enough, Hall confessed to everything and led police to the graves of his victims. The murder of Coggle was connected to Hall after he confessed to killing her. After a failed suicide attempt, Hall realised he was in for a lengthy sentence.

He also confessed that he had planned to kill Kitto, which is why he was acting fidgety at the hotel that night. Throughout 1978, both men appeared at different trials in Scotland and England, as the murders had taken place in two separate countries.

Hall was ultimately convicted of four murders and confirmed to have murdered Dorothy but her case didn't go to trial as the judge said it would not have affected the ultimate outcome of life imprisonment. Kitto was sentenced to life for three murders.

As time progressed and parole dates beckoned, various home secretaries ordered that Hall remain in prison under a whole life tariff. Hall published a biography called 'The Perfect Gentleman' in 1999 and died of natural causes in Kingston Prison, Portsmouth, in 2002, aged 78.

Hall was the oldest prisoner to be serving a whole life tariff when he died. Michael Kitto was released after his minimum term of 15 years in prison, in 1992. What happened to him afterwards is not public knowledge, but it is suspected he was set up with a new identity to live out the rest of his days in freedom.

The West's

A cruel tale of serial killing, abuse, and Britain's most evil couple, Fred and Rose West, who buried the bodies of their victims under the patio in their garden.

Fred West, in league with his wife, Rosemary West, would take the lives of at least 12 young women before being arrested in 1994. Their address of 25 Cromwell Street became synonymous with the murders and became known as the House of Horrors in the British press.

So much public hate was subsequently directed towards the House of Horrors, that Gloucester City Council intervened. They purchased the property for £40,000 in 1996, in the knowledge that no one would live there. They then unceremoniously destroyed the property, and with it, any physical trace of the horrors that had haunted the building.

During their uniquely evil relationship, Fred and Rose buried the remains of nine victims under their patio in the garden of 25 Cromwell Street, including their daughter, Heather. Fred's eight-year-old stepdaughter was unearthed at his previous home in Midland Road, Gloucester.

Fred's first wife and a childminder were found buried in shallow graves in remote locations outside the city limits. The 12 victims in total are the ones we know about, whose lives were ended in the most horrific of ways, with many being decapitated and dismembered. Police have long suspected that the bones of further victims are buried in and around Gloucester.

The formation of evil

Fred West was born in 1941 and raised during World War Two, the first child to a family of poor farm workers in Herefordshire. His father was strict and his mother overprotective, leading to him becoming known as a mummy's boy.

By 1951, the West's had six surviving children, as two had died within months of being born. Each of the children were given chores on the farm but Fred developed a habit of thieving. His mother sexually abused him and forced him to engage in sex acts with animals in his early teen years. His father also had open sexual relationships with Fred's younger sisters, which instilled a notion in Fred that incest was normal.

At the age of 17, a year after leaving school, he crashed his motorbike and remained unconscious for a week in hospital with a fractured skull and many broken bones. From then, he became prone to fits of extreme rage and anger.

In 1961, when he was 20, his 13-year-old sister, Kitty, told her parents that Fred had been raping her since she was 12. As word got around, Fred was arrested, but told police that he had been raping and sexually abusing young girls because it was a normal thing to do and everybody did it. The case was thrown out when Kitty refused to testify.

From then, Fred was abandoned by his family, and so he sought to create his own. He married his first wife, Catherine Bernadette Costello, in November 1962 at an empty wedding ceremony. Catherine gave birth to a mix-raced child, Charmaine, from her first relationship and Fred's first daughter, Anna Marie in 1964.

While living in Glasgow, the West's nanny, Isa McNeill, said the two girls were kept in cages on their bunk beds and only let out when Fred was at work. In 1965, Fred ran over and killed a young boy with his ice cream van but it was considered an accident and he was freed of any wrongdoing. A few months later, he took Charmaine and Anna Marie to his new home, a rented caravan in Gloucester.

Fred had met his first murder victim, Ann McFall, in Glasgow when she was 16, a friend of the nanny. By the time she was 18, she was living in

Fred's caravan and was pregnant with his child. While she was pregnant, she disappeared and was never seen again – until June 1994, when her remains were unearthed in a cornfield. It was suggested her unborn child was cut from her womb as she was still alive.

Crossing of dark souls

In 1969, the then 29-year-old Fred, met 15-year-old Rosemary Letts at a bus stop, and over the coming months, after showering her with gifts, she moved into his caravan as an informal nanny to Anna Marie and Charmaine. Rose's family disapproved of the relationship, including her father, Bill Letts, who was diagnosed with schizophrenia. And yet, Rose's path to evil had also been marred by abuse.

When Rose's mother was pregnant with her, she underwent electroconvulsive therapy for her depression, which some say caused prenatal injuries to Rose. From the age of 14, Rose would walk around the house naked and was known to have abused her two younger brothers. It was also claimed but never proven that Rose was raped by her own father in her formative years, which caused her to abuse her siblings.

Fred was imprisoned in December 1970 for the theft of car tyres and remained in prison until June 1971. Rose gave birth to their first child together, Heather, a few months before. During Fred's sentence, while in their new flat at Midland Road, Gloucester, Charmaine and Anna Marie were subjected to physical and sexual abuse from Rose. A few days before Fred's release, Rose killed Charmaine and stored her body in the coal cellar.

When Fred was released, he cut off Charmaine's fingers and buried the body in the back yard of the block of flats. Later on, it would remain unclear for a while who exactly had killed Charmaine but evidence proved that Fred West was serving his sentence at the time of her death.

In August 1971, Catherine went to Gloucester to confront Fred about the custody of her children and was never seen alive again. Her body was uncovered many years later in a small wood. She had been dismembered and the body parts placed into different plastic bags. As with most of Fred's victims, her fingers had been removed, and likely kept by him as mementos of the crimes.

Murdering as a pair

By January 1972, when Rose was pregnant with their second child, the West's moved into 25 Cromwell Street, a rented council property that Fred later purchased from the council for around £7,000. As part of the purchase, he turned the upper floor rooms into bedsits to take lodgers to help pay for the ever-growing West family. Rose and Fred married at the end of the same month and gave birth to Mae June in the Summer.

Over the years, Rose turned to prostitution and used a room in the house to entertain her clients, complete with peepholes that allowed Fred – and his children – to watch. By 1983, Rose had given birth to eight children, some of them black, as they were the offspring of some of her clients. Many of the children were killed by her and Fred.

At least eight of the victims had been raped, tortured, and mutilated. Before being murdered, they were used in violent sexual fantasies where bondage played a heavy part in the household. They would then dismember the bodies and bury them in the cellar and garden of 25 Cromwell Street.

Before Cromwell Street, Fred had killed two on his own and Rosemary killed one; Charmaine. The rest of their victims were killed as a pair. The level of control they asserted over others is as horrific as it is shocking. Rose would also engage in casual sex with both male and female lodgers. It was stated that when she had sex with other women, Rose would become more violent as the control slipped. She would partially suffocate them and insert exceptionally large sex objects inside them.

If they cried or showed fear or pain then Rose would become more excited. Shockingly, when

Rose's father found out about her prostitution, he would regularly visit her to have sex with his own daughter. It was clear that both Fred and Rose took to extreme levels of sexual perversity, and it was this that resulted in the deaths of so many.

Fred West also collected VHS videos that showed bestiality and child abuse. It has always remained unclear how he was sourcing these types of tapes but they were surely a catalyst to even more crimes. Since the marriage in 1972, the sexual violence increased. It became shocking to many that the crimes were going mostly unseen in what was a busy residential street.

Everybody does it

All of the West's children were abused in some form or another. They took 'great care' not to mark the children's faces or hands when they assaulted them. Any admittance to hospitals were explained away as accidents and never reported. All the children witnessed the abuse inflicted on each other and regular sexual abuse became the norm.

From the age of eight, Anna Marie, Fred's daughter via Catherine, was subjected to horrific abuse. She was dragged to the cellar of 25 Cromwell Street and had her clothes torn off. She was tied naked to a mattress and gagged before Fred raped her as Rose egged him on – this became a regular occurrence.

"Everybody does it to every girl. It's a father's job. Don't say anything to anybody." - Rose West, to Anna Marie.

They would then sexually abuse Anna Marie at any time from then on, by tying her to various items of furniture and forcing her into degrading acts. Fred would rape her regularly and then force her to do her chores while wearing a mini-skirt adorned with adult sexual devices.

When Anna Marie was 13, she was forced to become a sex worker in 'Rose's Room' with Rose watching every encounter with clients in case Anna Marie revealed her true age. Anna Marie was only one of the children – others would suffer even worse fates at the hands of Fred and Rose.

"I made you, I can do what I like with you." – Fred West, to his daughters.

They killed 12 young women between them, mostly their daughters, or hitchhikers who ended up at the house. In 1987, they killed their daughter, Heather West, and buried her under the patio of their garden. Fred even put a wooden table over her makeshift grave, a table where he would have family dinners outside in the Summer. The other children didn't know their sister was beneath them as they dined.

Uncovering the horrors

In 1973, a lodger at the house was tied up and subjected to abuse but she managed to escape while visiting a launderette. The West's were arrested for assault and rape but were released free of charge when the lodger refused to appear at the trial. The West's were let off with a £50 fine.

20 years later in 1993, the West's were arrested again when one of their daughters spoke out about the abuse but she too refused to testify in court. The West's were freed but their five remaining children were taken into foster care. While looking at the abuse case, investigators reopened the investigation into the disappearance of Heather West, who disappeared in 1987.

It was the reopening of the case that would ultimately lead investigators to uncover the horrors surrounding the West's and would lead to their arrest. It was the excavation of the patio after their arrest that led to multiple bodies and body parts being uncovered. The investigation found remains in the ground floor bathroom, multiple bodies in the cellar and a large number in the garden.

Each body had been heavily mutilated and had been subjected to extremely violent sexual abuse before their deaths. They found severed limbs, a skull, knives and various bondage materials. Bizarrely, every one of the human remains were missing some of their bones, most notably the phalange bones, which are the bones found in the fingers. Heather's remains were found in the same location. In total, the remains of nine victims were found at 25 Cromwell Street.

Initially, Rose denied murdering any victims and claimed to be a victim of Fred's but Fred confessed that she had helped in dismembering the corpses. In the instance of the death of one of their lodgers, Shirley Robinson, Rose had removed a foetus from her womb and put it in a plastic bag for burial in their garden.

Horrific legacy

Heather's death in 1987, was considered the West's final murder victim, and Fred would tell his surviving children – and sex slaves – that if they didn't follow orders that they would end up under the patio like Heather. At their trial, it materialised that Fred and Rose had made a pact where Fred would claim responsibility for all the murders to let Rose get away with it.

However, the investigation into the murders discovered that Rose was instrumental in some of them, and she was charged the same as Fred. On 30th June 1994, Fred was charged with 12 murders, and Rose with nine. Fred was also charged with the murder of Anne McFall, whose body had been found a couple of weeks earlier but not identified at the time.

On New Year's Day 1995, while awaiting trial, Fred killed himself in his prison cell by turning his blanket into a rope and hanging himself. In November 1995, Rose was convicted of ten murders and sentenced to life in prison without the possibility of parole. To this day, she continues to maintain her innocence.

During his interviews before his death, Fred West claimed to have killed 30 people, 20 with Rose, and was going to reveal the location of one body every year to investigators, claiming they were spread around Gloucester under paving stones. Since then, other crimes have been tentatively linked to him but have not been confirmed, including seven rapes in the 1970s. The fingers of his victims have never been found.

Rose West receives only one sole visitor; Anna Marie. In 1999, Anna Marie attempted suicide but was saved by a friend. One of the West's sons; Stephen, also attempted suicide in 2002. Later, in 2004, Stephen was jailed for having sex with a 14-year-old girl. It appears that the West's horrific legacy will ultimately continue to be felt.

Exorcism Turned Loving Husband into Killer

A loving husband, thought to be possessed by 40 demons, became the subject of an all-night exorcism, and less than two hours later; ripped his wife and dog to pieces with his bare hands.

xorcism turned loving husband into killer! A true case of possession! The Ossett exorcist murder! So read the headlines in 1974 England, when 31-year-old Michael Taylor killed his wife by tearing her eyes and tongue out with his bare hands, following an exorcism by a local team of priests.

Born at the tail-end of the Second World War in 1944, Michael was raised in the English market town of Ossett in Wakefield, West Yorkshire. Though Ossett was very much a Christian town, the Taylor family were not overly religious and never found the time to attend the local churches.

Neighbours of the family described them as mild-mannered and full of kindness, despite their unwillingness for a religious life. Michael became a full-time butcher and married the love of his life, Christine, soon after.

By the early 1970s, the couple had five children and were living in a small rustic house in the town they'd both grown up in with their dog. Michael hurt his back in an accident that forced him to leave the butcher's job and struggled to find full-time employment afterwards.

He suffered bouts of depression which saw him becoming withdrawn from the community and he became less social with those around him. This caught the attention of one of his friends, Barbara Wardman, who believed the only cure for his depression was religion.

Carnal desire

Barbara introduced him to a church group called the Gawber Christian Fellowship, despite Michael not attending church regularly. He attended the first group meeting with Christine, and both were so impressed with the group's outlook on life that they converted straight away.

When Michael's depression began to improve after a number of group meetings, his friends and members of the church believed it had improved purely on the basis of spiritual intervention and by the hand of God himself.

While at the church meetings, Michael became besotted with the 20-year-old lay preacher, Marie

Robinson. A lay preacher is a preacher or religious servant who is not a formally ordained cleric and helps the church in the promotion and function of its beliefs.

Within a few months, their friendship had reportedly become 'carnal' – another way of saying they were intimately engaged. Marie's soft spoken leadership of the group was too much for Michael to ignore and he spent as much time with her as he could.

Soon enough, Marie held private meetings with Michael, where he would supposedly talk in tongues and made the sign of the cross with his hands for hours on end, believing it would quieten the dark and evil power of the moon; the opposite to the light and goodness of the sun.

Michael began joining in some of the sermons and helped cast out demons from other group members, even though neither Marie nor Michael were trained exorcists. They were simply using their positions to empower themselves.

A few weeks later, members of the group met at Michael's home, and Christine voiced her opinion that Michael was spending too much time with Marie. Michael then forced Marie upstairs where she rejected his advances before re-joining the group.

The exorcism

When Marie rejected him in his own home, Michael's attitude changed and he became argumentative with Christine at every opportunity. He withdrew back into depression, acted irrationally and developed a bad attitude towards the church group.

Then Michael attacked Marie in full view of the group. He rose from his seat, and stared at her with wild, bestial eyes, and a look of a man intent on killing. Marie began screaming out of fear at the sight of him but Michael grabbed her by the shoulders and neck and shouted at her in tongues.

Marie called upon the name of Jesus, and the other members of the group managed to restrain Michael, who had no memory of what had gone down. Concerned he was becoming possessed by a demon, the congregation called on a local priest and his wife to intervene.

Peter and Sally Vincent invited Michael to their home for an assessment where Michael threw their cat out of a window and broke some pottery in anger. After witnessing his anger and actions, the Vincent's put together a team of people to help in an exorcism at the church.

On 5th October 1974, as the midnight hour dawned, Michael was summoned to St. Thomas Church where he was restrained and underwent a seven-hour exorcism. Peter and his team burned Michael's crucifix, pushed wooden crosses into his mouth, doused him with holy water and screamed at him to dispel the demons.

At the court case following the murder, Peter confirmed they had exorcised a total of 40 demons who had taken residence within Michael.

Coincidentally, the only demons they couldn't exorcise were those associated with murder, violence, and insanity.

Ripped at and left in a mess

The priests told Michael not to worry about the other three demons and that they would exorcise them at a later date, so he was sent home. Less than two hours later, a policeman on a routine patrol through the town stumbled on a gruesome sight.

Michael was ambling along the street completely naked and covered head to toe in blood, screaming about the demons within him and Satan himself. The officer managed to restrain Michael and took him to a hospital, before heading to Michael's home where more police were outside.

Their neighbours had heard violent noises and already called police. When the officer arrived, a senior detective stumbled out the house and vomited in the front garden, telling him not to go inside as Christine Taylor had been ripped at and left in a mess.

In a possessed rage, Michael had killed his wife by tearing at her face and chest with his bare hands. He ripped out her eyes and tongue, and according to the autopsy report, had almost ripped off her entire face from her skull.

He had then strangled the family dog to death before tearing its body to pieces, ripping its limbs off and covering himself in its blood, along with the walls and floor. When Michael was arrested in hospital, he claimed that *'the evil inside her had been destroyed.'*

Torment of the exorcism

In an unprecedented trial, Michael was acquitted on the grounds of insanity. A defence psychologist posited the theory that Michael's actions were a direct result of the intense psychological torment he had suffered at the exorcism, and laid blame on the priests involved.

The priests who were brought in to testify stated they had expelled all but three of the demons and it was one of the three demons that had possessed Michael and used his body to kill Christine. Though the trial didn't prove that Michael was possessed, it did lead to him being acquitted.

Michael was sent to the infamous Broadmoor psychiatric hospital for two years before being transferred to a lower-security facility for another two. He was released just four years after brutally murdering his wife and dog.

If any of this sounds familiar, the case was mentioned in the 2021 film *The Conjuring: The Devil Made Me Do It*, which is based on the 1981 trial of American murderer Arne Cheyenne Johnson, who claimed he was possessed by a demon.

The case was investigated by demonologists Ed and Lorraine Warren, who believed that Arne was indeed possessed. Arne was ultimately convicted of manslaughter and spent five years in prison. Demonic possession was never proven.

The exorcism of Michael Taylor raised many public questions that were never answered including why the priests in charge of the exorcism had never been charged with psychological damage, or why Michael was released only four years later.

Whether he was possessed, psychologically tortured, mentally unstable, or a cold-blooded killer, depends on one's own beliefs of the existence of the otherworldly, and that which can inhabit a human body and mind.

In 2005, Michael was arrested again for touching a teenage girl, and was admitted to psychiatric care – with the same symptoms as he had showed in the hours before he ripped his wife apart. Leading some researchers to suspect that a demon remains within him still.

Look for more in the Orrible British True Crime Series!

OUT NOW!

For bibliographies, citations, true crime blog posts, more true crime books, and more information on new releases for your collection, head on over to www.benoakley.co.uk